# ATLAS *of*
# IRISH
# HISTORY

# ATLAS *of* IRISH HISTORY

Seán Duffy

Gabriel Doherty

Raymond Gillespie

James Kelly

Colm Lennon

Brendan Smith

MACMILLAN

MACMILLAN USA
A Simon & Schuster Macmillan Company
1633 Broadway
New York, NY 10019–6785

Library of Congress Cataloging-in-Publication Data

The Macmillan atlas of Irish history / Seán Duffy, editor.
        p.    cm.
    Includes bibliographical references and index.
    ISBN 0-02-862011-9
    1. Ireland—History.        I. Duffy, Seán.
    DA911.M26  1997
    941.5—DC21                                              97-28623
                                                                CIP


Manufactured in the United Kingdom
10 9 8 7 6 5 4 3 2 1

# Contributors

**Seán Duffy** lectures in Medieval Irish and British history in Trinity College, Dublin.

**Gabriel Doherty** teaches in the Department of History, University College, Cork.

**Raymond Gillespie** teaches in the Department of History at St Patrick's College, Maynooth.

**James Kelly** teaches in the Department of History at St Patrick's College, Drumcondra, Dublin.

**Colm Lennon** teaches in the Department of History at St Patrick's College, Maynooth.

**Brendan Smith** teaches history in the Department of Historical Studies at the University of Bristol.

# Foreword

Out on the western edge of Europe, a first glance at the map makes Ireland seem a small and isolated place. However, many peoples have by turns established themselves on this remote island, creating an historical dynamic whose dispersed voices are now heard in almost every major city of the globe, in accents unmistakably from Cork or Connemara, Donegal or Dublin. This atlas attempts to explain in a visual, accessible way Ireland's unfolding story, and how this small country's remarkable worldwide impact has come about.

Some ten millennia ago, the first people arrived in Ireland, perhaps across the land bridge that once linked Ireland to Scotland, and began the region's human story. Not much more than two millennia ago arrived the ancestors of the Gaels, who after hundreds of years of assimilation and adaptation gave and continue to give the island its distinct identity.

Over the past thousand years, the Vikings, Normans, English and Scots have all left their mark on Ireland's culture, religion, language and landscape. They have also left schisms which survive to this day. For more than 800 years, Ireland's history was by degrees tied to that of England, moving from the margins of English royal interests to the status of a colony. From 1800 the island was governed directly from Westminster, with Irish soldiers guarding the Asian frontiers of Britain's global empire, Irish workers building bridges in Africa, and Irish settlers roaming the Canadian prairies. While the Irishman's wanderlust has never been in doubt, not all of this dispersion however, was of Ireland's choosing.

Ireland's desire to set its own direction surfaced many times, and by the 1920s most of the island had secured its independence, with the exception of the northeast corner which remained within the United Kingdom. This partition, and its ramifications for both the southern state and Great Britain, continue to be hotly contested and debated, as the newspapers daily and often tragically remind us.

The maps and texts of this atlas are intended to spotlight the movements of Ireland's long and multi-layered history and to explain how its present circumstances have arisen. Maps tend to show facts rather than influences or ideas, and as such are simply snapshots in time. This collection, however, is accompanied by text written by some of the leading authorities in the field, and it is hoped that, together, these contributions will go some way to explain the story of this unique and fascinating place.

Seán Duffy
For the authors

# Contents

# PART I: ORIGINS

*Seán Duffy*

FAINT TRACES of human food-gathering and hunting survive in Ireland from the Mesolithic period (perhaps as early as 8,000 BC). These early people may have migrated from Britain, though hardly before the land-bridge between the islands was washed away, and such weapons and tools as they have left behind are mostly small flint blades. They lived on wild pig, small mammals, fowl, fish and edible plants, and dwelt in small huts in isolated bands and hunting camps, perhaps migrating seasonally. The island must have been sparsely inhabited, and has yielded no evidence of artistic activity, or of agriculture.

Above: *The chamber of the passage tomb at Newgrange, Co. Meath. The massive uprights are parts of the estimated 200,000 ton of stones transported to the site during its construction.*

Ireland's first crop-growers and live-stock-breeders were Neolithic peoples who arrived by sea from Britain or the Continent about 6,000 years ago. It was they who made the first real impact on Ireland's land-scape, building more substantial houses and stone boundary walls. Their pottery and decoration developed, and there is evidence of 'industrial' activity in the form of the large-scale manufacture of axes. They also constructed numerous megalithic monuments such as passage-tombs, court-cairns and dolmens, used for burial and for ritualistic and cultic purposes. These are among the earliest examples of true architecture known anywhere in the world and many survive in the Irish landscape today, some preserving examples of advanced mural art.

During the Bronze Age (*c.* 2,500–600 BC) Ireland's first metal-workers, not necessarily new immigrants, exploited the island's rich copper deposits to produce copper and bronze axe- and spear-heads, and later, shields, cauldrons, sickles and craftsmen's tools. Their legacy includes beautiful personal ornaments, many in gold, such as earrings, fibulae (dress fasteners) and lunulae (an item of neck or hair jewellery, shaped like a half-moon). Later they produced a great variety of highly accomplished neck, arm and waist ornaments, the prehistoric goldsmiths' craft probably reaching its peak at about 700 BC. In fact, more gold-crafted objects survive from this period in Ireland than in any other country in western or northern Europe, and some objects of Irish type have been found in Britain and the continent, suggesting an active export trade. From this period, too, may belong the many stone circles and 'wedge' tombs throughout the countryside. Pottery used for food and funerary urns also reached a high standard.

By about 600 BC iron had come to replace bronze as the main source-material for weapons and tools, and it was during the ensuing Iron Age that the first

Celtic peoples appeared in Ireland. They have left us the Irish language and art-work in the La Tène style associated with the Celts of central Europe. By the beginning of this period great hilltop enclosures like Tara and Emain Macha were in use, sites which sometimes also had an earlier importance. Though evidence is scanty, some cliff-top 'promontory forts' may date from this era, as may some 'crannóg' lake-dwellings. The Roman invasion of Britain affected Ireland to the extent that trading contacts with the Empire were enhanced, and Ireland may have provided a haven for refugees from the conquest and a base from which to raid western Britain. As the Roman Empire declined, unrelated Irish colonies took root in what are now Wales and Cornwall and in western Scotland, the last being ultimately of greatest influence. It was probably in this period that the 'ring-fort' became established as the home of wealthy farmers, those with earthen banks usually being called 'raths' and those with stone walls, 'cashels'. Thousands of these still dot the countryside and many remained in use well into the historic period.

The historic period begins with the introduction of Christianity in the 5th century, and Ireland first emerges into the light of history in documents ascribed to the British missionary, St. Patrick. Thereafter it developed a highly literate society which has left a substantial corpus of literature in both Latin and Irish, allowing us to form a mental picture of Dark-Age Ireland that is clearer and far more detailed than that offered by most other European countries. Using annals, genealogies, king lists and other sources, we can assemble the names of the many peoples who dominated the island, the territories they held, and the rise and fall of their various dynasties. Other sources allow us to plot the progress of Christianity in the country, in which, by the mid-6th century, monks and monasteries had eclipsed bishops and dioceses, their houses becoming centers not just of piety, but of learning, study and art. The members of the monastic communities studied the Bible, the writings of the early Church Fathers, canon law and Latin grammar. They copied manuscripts, many of them beautifully illuminated, and commissioned masterpieces of metalwork and carved stone. As the monastic ideal flourished, earning Ireland the name 'island of saints,' their missionaries spread to Britain and the continent, followed by scholars and teachers in what was truly a 'Golden Age'.

The 7th- and 8th-century law tracts, heavily influenced by the Scriptures, portray a society that was intensely hierarchical, where status and honor meant much, and where sharp distinctions were drawn between those regarded as 'sacred' (including kings, clerics and poets) and those who were not, and between the free and the unfree. On the highest rungs of the ladder stood the kings, around whom society revolved. Ireland was a land of many kings, the tracts defining three grades: kings of petty local kingdoms, over-kings ruling several of these, and 'kings of over-kings' who effectively ruled a whole province. Although the laws rarely refer to a high-king of all Ireland, it is clear that for much of the early historic period the leading dynasty, the Uí Néill, who were based in the northern half of the country, with their ceremonial capital at Tara, did claim, and were occasionally able to enforce, supremacy throughout the island. Their primacy was shattered in the early 11th century, and power then revolved around a half-dozen or so leading province-kings, each of whom sought to force his rivals into submission and make himself high-king.

It is difficult to assess the extent to which these changes were the result of the Viking incursions, which for a time in the 9th century appeared likely to over-whelm the country. The Vikings certainly increased the intensity of warfare in an already violent society, and by developing towns at Dublin, Waterford, Limerick, Wexford and Cork, and trading networks overseas, they added to the wealth of what was otherwise a largely pastoral economy. Their presence in strength in Munster no doubt contributed also to the decline of its reigning dynasty, the Eóganachta, and facilitated the rise of Brian Boru. His later fame was attributed to a notable victory over the Vikings at the Battle of Clontarf in 1014, but his real importance lies in the fact that he ended the monopoly on the high-kingship formerly held by the Uí Néill.

In time, the Viking enclaves were assimilated into the Irish political super-structure, and those Irish kings who succeeded in dominating them, in some cases establishing the Viking town as their capital, gained an advantage over their rivals in the race for the high-kingship. This was especially true in the case of Dublin, overlordship of which was by the late 10th century generally assert-ed by successful claimants to the high-kingship and which, by the mid-11th cen-tury, was directly ruled by Irish kings, effectively becoming the country's capital.

This period saw rapid changes in Ireland in both Church and state. The Gregorian reform movement, which sought to eradicate abuses in the Church throughout western Christendom, spread to Ireland by the early 12th century and, under the patronage of reform-minded Irish province-kings, was responsi-ble for major changes in the organization of the Irish Church, though it was considerably less successful in eradicating abuses in Church practice and moral laxities among the laity. In secular affairs, the same period witnessed what may have been the evolution of a national monarchy, as a series of ambitious province-kings steadily increased their powers, started to act as feudal lords in the European mode, and sought to stamp their authority throughout the island. This, however, was cut short in the late 12th century by the Anglo-Norman inva-sion, spearheaded by men from the Welsh borderlands. They came at the insti-gation of the Leinster king, Diarmait MacMurchada (Dermot MacMurrough), who had been expelled by the reigning high-king, Ruaidrí Ua Conchobair (Rory O'Connor). The invaders were led by Richard de Clare, better known as Strongbow, who married MacMurchada's daughter and later succeeded to Leinster. At this point, late in 1171, Henry II, who had earlier received a papal licence to invade Ireland in order, it was claimed, to aid in the process of Church reform, came to Ireland himself, the first English king ever to do so, and estab-lished the English lordship.

*Right: From* The Book of Kells: *'the Arrest of Christ,' The manuscript is one of the supreme examples of Irish art, drawing on the work and development of earlier monastic art. The use of color and designs around the strong image of man are some of the qualities which make this work unique.*

# Celtic Ireland

IN THE SECOND half of the first millennium BC, during what prehistorians call the Iron Age, the first Celtic peoples began to arrive in Ireland, though there is no surviving evidence of a large-scale invasion. The people known to the Greeks as Keltoi, or Celts, had dominated central and western Europe and spoke an Indo-European language which developed into P-Celtic, the language of Britain and Gaul, ancestor of Welsh and Breton, and Q-Celtic, the language of the Celtic inhabitants of Ireland, ancestor of Gaelic.

Celtic culture of this period is called La Tène after a site in Switzerland, and objects in the La Tène style survive mainly from the north and west of Ireland. Best known are the Turoe Stone in County Galway, some beautifully crafted war trumpets, golden collars, or *torcs*, and decorated bronze scabbards and horse bits. These objects seem to have belonged to a warrior society and their prevalence in Connacht and Ulster may be significant, for the latter is the setting of the *Táin Bó Cuailnge* and other great sagas of the Irish heroic age. These tales were written considerably later and should be used with caution, but they do capture something of the society that was thought to exist in Ireland in the immediate prehistoric period, a society not unlike that portrayed by contemporary descriptions of the continental Celts.

The earliest detailed account of Ireland is that by Ptolemy, an Alexandrian Greek geographer writing after AD 100, whose information may have come from Roman or British sailors familiar with the island's east coast and its main rivers, fifteen of which Ptolemy notes. Of the peoples whose territories Ptolemy records, we can probably identify Dál Riata of Antrim (who were soon to found a powerful kingdom in Argyll), Dál Fiatach of Down, and Ulaid, who were later confined to Antrim and Down, though Ptolemy has them still ruling much of the north from their cult center at Emain Macha. Emain Macha was the setting of much of the action of the early saga literature.

As Ptolemy moves from the northeast, it becomes harder to match his territories with known dynasties, and he makes no mention of the massive Iron-Age earthworks at Tara, County Meath, perhaps the most important of the early royal and ritual sites. It does seem likely, though, that the *Iverni*, whom Ptolemy places in the southwest, may be the Érainn, who dominated Munster in this period: the Greek name for Ireland, *Ierne*, probably came from them, and is itself a version of the Irish word for the island, *Ériu* (later, *Éire*).

*Below: The Turoe Stone, Co. Galway, is probably of La Tène period. Its purpose is unknown, though most likely to be of religious significance.*

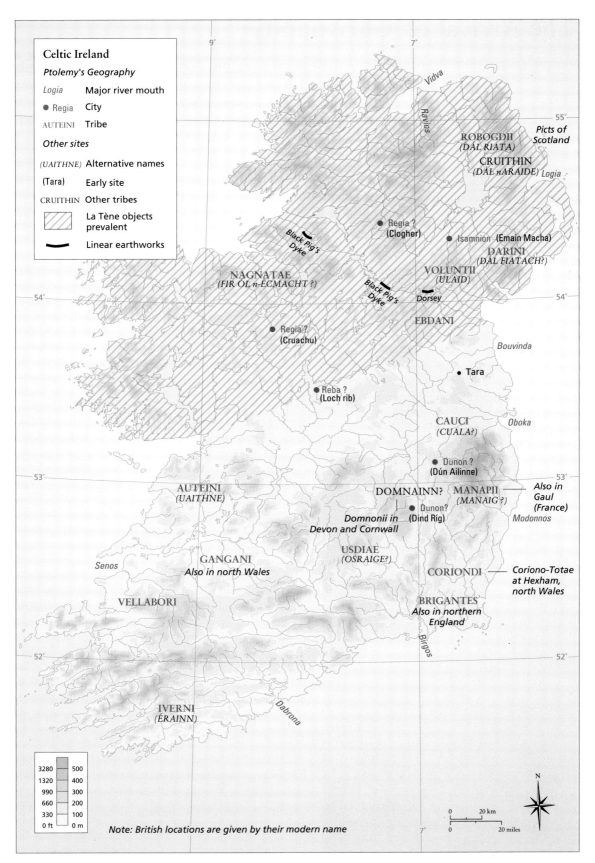

**Celtic Ireland**

*Ptolemy's Geography*

| | |
|---|---|
| *Logia* | Major river mouth |
| ● *Regia* | City |
| AUTEINI | Tribe |

*Other sites*

| | |
|---|---|
| (*UAITHNE*) | Alternative names |
| (Tara) | Early site |
| CRUITHIN | Other tribes |
| ▨ | La Tène objects prevalent |
| ▬ | Linear earthworks |

*Vidva*

*Ravios*

ROBOGDII
(*DÁL RIATA*)

Picts of Scotland

CRUITHIN
(*DÁL nARAIDE*)

*Logia*

● Regia ?
(Clogher)

● Isamnion  (Emain Macha)

DARINI
(*DÁL FIATACH?*)

Black Pig's Dyke

NAGNATAE
(*FIR ÓL n-ECMACHT ?*)

Black Pig's Dyke

VOLUNTII
(*ULAID*)

Dorsey

EBDANI

● Regia ?
(Cruachu)

*Bouvinda*

● Tara

● Reba ?
(Loch ríb)

CAUCI
(*CUALA?*)

*Oboka*

● Dúnon ?
(Dún Ailinne)

AUTEINI
(*UAITHNE*)

DOMNAINN?

MANAPII
(*MANAIG ?*)

Also in Gaul (France)

● Dunon?
(Dind Ríg)

*Modonnos*

Domnonii in Devon and Cornwall

USDIAE
(*OSRAIGE?*)

GANGANI
Also in north Wales

CORIONDI

Coriono-Totae at Hexham, north Wales

*Senos*

VELLABORI

BRIGANTES
Also in northern England

*Birgos*

IVERNI
(*ÉRAINN*)

*Dabrona*

| | |
|---|---|
| 3280 | 500 |
| 1320 | 400 |
| 990 | 300 |
| 660 | 200 |
| 330 | 100 |
| 0 ft | 0 m |

N

0      20 km

0      20 miles

*Note: British locations are given by their modern name*

# The Arrival of Christianity

ALTHOUGH Ireland lay outside the Roman Empire, it was heavily influenced by it, and evidence of trading is considerable. As Roman power in Britain weakened, by the early 5th century the Irish were not only trading and raiding there, but settling along its western coast, most successfully the Dál Riata colony in what became Scotland, but also a Déisi colony in south Wales, a Laigin (Leinster) colony in north Wales, and settlement by the Uí Liatháin in Cornwall and Devon. Such contacts with the Roman world produced the Ogham script, consisting of notches on stone based on the Latin alphabet. No doubt they also produced the first Irish encounters with Christianity.

*Below: This stone from Coolmagort, Co. Kerry, displays Ogham inscriptions, the earliest written Irish.*

The first Christian missionaries may have come to Ireland from Gaul in the late 4th and early 5th centuries, making it the first country outside the Roman world to be converted. The first exact date is 431, the year in which Palladius, possibly a deacon of Auxerre, was appointed by the Pope as bishop to 'the Irish who believe in Christ'. Gaulish missionaries, whose labors were probably confined largely to the east and south of Ireland, were soon superseded by British, the most famous of whom is the still highly controversial St. Patrick. Patrick himself states that he was the son of an official in a city in Roman Britain, and that he was first brought to Ireland as a slave, but later returned as a bishop to preach the gospel. He was most active, it seems, north of a line from Wexford to Galway, and was particularly successful in the northeast; it was a church in this area, Armagh, because of its alleged association with Patrick, that was later to claim primacy over the rest of the Irish Church.

The cult which grew up around Patrick should not mislead us into thinking that the conversion of Ireland was quick, or largely the work of one man. We do not known anything of the activities of Palladius, but later accounts give the names of other bishops active at this period. Auxilius is said to have founded Killashee (*Cill Usailli*) near Naas, one of the royal sites associated with the kings of Leinster, while Dunshaughlin, not far from Tara, is attributed to Secundinus: in Irish it is *Domnach Sechnaill*, and sites with the element *domnach* (from Latin *dominicum*) are known to be early. Like these other early churches, Armagh is near the revered site at Emain Macha, in each case suggesting a deliberate policy of locating the new Christian churches beside old pre-Christian power-centers.

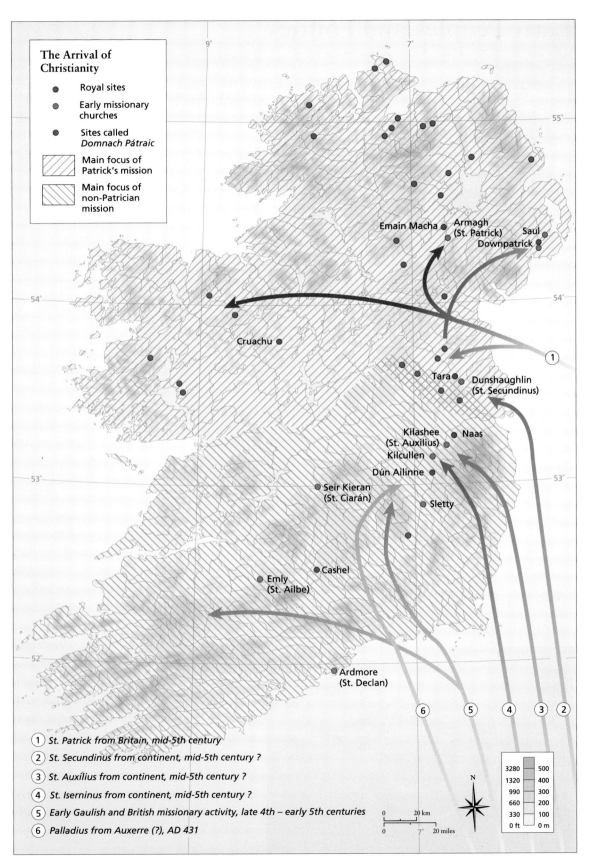

The Arrival of
Christianity

- Royal sites
- Early missionary churches
- Sites called *Domnach Pátraic*
- Main focus of Patrick's mission
- Main focus of non-Patrician mission

Emain Macha
Armagh (St. Patrick)
Saul
Downpatrick

Cruachu

Tara
Dunshaughlin (St. Secundinus)

Kilashee (St. Auxilius)
Naas
Kilcullen
Dún Ailinne

Seir Kieran (St. Ciarán)
Sletty

Cashel

Emly (St. Ailbe)

Ardmore (St. Declan)

① St. Patrick from Britain, mid-5th century
② St. Secundinus from continent, mid-5th century ?
③ St. Auxilius from continent, mid-5th century ?
④ St. Iserninus from continent, mid-5th century ?
⑤ Early Gaulish and British missionary activity, late 4th – early 5th centuries
⑥ Palladius from Auxerre (?), AD 431

N

0    20 km

0    20 miles

| 3280 | 500 |
| 1320 | 400 |
| 990 | 300 |
| 660 | 200 |
| 330 | 100 |
| 0 ft | 0 m |

# Early Peoples and Politics

Above: *Detail of a bearded warrior with spear and shield, from* The Book of Kells.

WITH THE introduction of Christianity in the 5th century came the Latin language, and with Latin came learning and literature, both in Latin and, increasingly, in the vernacular. This material, the most comprehensive to survive in any country of Dark-Age Europe, enables us to reconstruct the political map of Ireland even at this early period. The first thing that emerges is the extent to which political divisions had changed since Ptolemy's time. By the 7th century, the Érainn peoples in Munster were eclipsed by a federation of dynasties known as the Eóganachta who traced their descent from the eponymous Eógan, and who may, as their later origin-legend claimed, have been Irish colonists returned from Britain: their capital was at Cashel, which is a borrowing of the Latin 'castellum.' To their east lay the over-kingdom of Laigin (Leinster), bounded on the west by the Barrow. Leinster originally stretched north to the Boyne, but it was pushed back to the Liffey after the 6th century, and was dominated by two dynasties, Uí Dúnlainge, centred on Kildare, and Uí Chennselaig, associated with Ferns.

The Laigin lost their lands in Meath to the Uí Néill, whose origins may lie to the west of the Shannon and who claimed descent from Niall Noígiallach ('Niall of the nine hostages'), a quasi-historical 5th-century figure. Connacht takes its name from a mythical ancestor of Niall, Conn Cétchathach ('Conn of the hundred battles'), and by the 8th century was dominated by two dynasties, Uí Briúin and Uí Fiachrach, allegedly descended from Bríon and Fiachra, brothers of Niall. By this period, Niall's reputed descendants held power in the northwest of Ireland, where they were known as the Northern Uí Néill, with a focal point at Ailech, and also in the midlands, where they are known as the Southern Uí Néill. Tara had been wrested by them from the Laigin, and the over-king of the Uí Néill bore the title 'King of Tara,' which in time came to denote the high-kingship of Ireland.

Below: *Tara, perhaps the most important site in Ireland archeologically, historically and symbolically, went through many phases of occupation over many centuries.*

As the Uí Néill and their subjects the Airgialla pushed north, they circumscribed the power of the Ulaid, who had earlier ruled as far south as the Boyne, defending the boundaries of their kingdom with massive linear earthworks, traces of which still survive. We do not know precisely when Emain Macha fell, but for most of the historic period the Ulaid's power was confined to the area east of the Bann, and their most important dynasty was Dál Fiatach, who ruled the Mournes from their capital at Downpatrick.

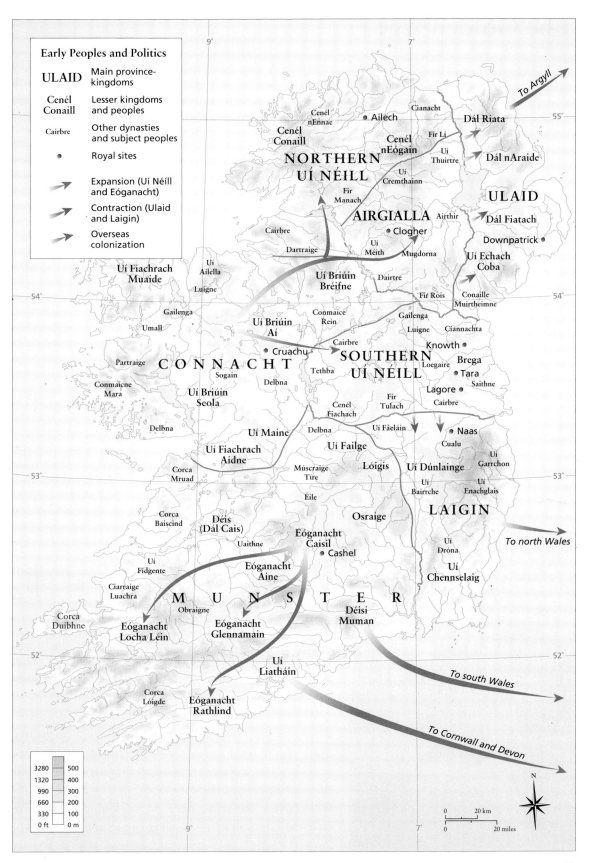

**Early Peoples and Politics**

**ULAID**  Main province-kingdoms

Cenél Conaill  Lesser kingdoms and peoples

Cairbre  Other dynasties and subject peoples

•  Royal sites

→  Expansion (Uí Néill and Eóganacht)

→  Contraction (Ulaid and Laigin)

→  Overseas colonization

To Argyll

Cenél nEnnae

• Ailech

Cianacht

Dál Riata

Cenél Conaill

**NORTHERN UÍ NÉILL**

Cenél nEógain

Fir Lí

Uí Thuirtre

Dál nAraide

Uí Cremthainn

**ULAID**

Fir Manach

**AIRGIALLA**  Airthir

Dál Fiatach

Cairbre

• Clogher

Downpatrick •

Dartraige

Uí Méith

Mugdorna

Uí Echach Coba

Uí Fiachrach Muaide

Uí Ailella

Uí Briúin Bréifne

Dairtre

Fir Rois

Conaille Muirtheimne

Luigne

Conmaice Rein

Gailenga

Gailenga

Umall

Uí Briúin Aí

Cairbre

Luigne

Ciannachta

Partraige

**C O N N A C H T**

Sogain

• Cruachu

Tethba

**SOUTHERN UÍ NÉILL**

Loegaire

Knowth •

**Brega**

Conmaicne Mara

Delbna

Delbna

• Tara

Saithne

Uí Briúin Seola

Cenél Fiachach

Fir Tulach

Lagore •

Cairbre

Delbna

Uí Maine

Delbna

Uí Fáeláin

• Naas

Corca Mruad

Uí Fiachrach Aidne

Múscraige Tíre

Uí Failge

Lóigis

Cualu

Uí Garrchon

Éile

Uí Dúnlainge

Uí Bairrche

Uí Enachglais

Corca Baiscind

Déis (Dál Cais)

Osraige

**L A I G I N**

To north Wales

Uaithne

Eóganacht Caisil

• Cashel

Uí Dróna

Uí Fidgente

Eóganacht Áine

Uí Chennselaig

Ciarraige Luachra

**M  U  N  S  T  E  R**

Déisi Muman

Corca Duibhne

Obraigne

Eóganacht Locha Léin

Eóganacht Glennamain

Corca Lóigde

Uí Liatháin

To south Wales

Eóganacht Rathlind

To Cornwall and Devon

| 3280 | 500 |
|------|-----|
| 1320 | 400 |
| 990 | 300 |
| 660 | 200 |
| 330 | 100 |
| 0 ft | 0 m |

N

0   20 km

0   20 miles

# The Golden Age

ALTHOUGH the beginnings of a diocesan structure may have been bequeathed to the Irish Church by the early missionaries, by the 6th century Ireland's most important churches were ruled by a monastic hierarchy, many of whom were not bishops, and certain monasteries which were believed to share a common founder were grouped together in what is known as a paruchia.

The original impetus for this wave of monasticism came partly from Britain. St. Enda, founder of Inis Mór, studied with St. Ninian in Galloway. The Welsh saints, David and Cadoc, were the inspiration for Máedóc of Ferns and Finnian of Clonard. Finnian then taught men who became important monastic founders in their own right, including Brendan (Clonfert), Ciarán (Clonmacnoise), and Colum Cille (Durrow, Derry and Iona). The monastic centers were not the exclusive preserve of men, the most famous house of nuns being St. Brigid's at Kildare, and while some churches were easily accessible and richly endowed, and undoubtedly places as much of commerce as of prayer, others, most notably Sceilg Mhicil off the Kerry coast, were retreats from the world.

This newly Christianized and literate society soon began to display evidence of a high level of scholarship, both in Latin and Irish, clerical and secular, all of it heavily influenced by the Church. By the 7th century, Ireland's monastic schools and libraries were well-stocked with the writings of the early Church Fathers, and were beginning to produce scholars and holy men of their own, whose work was comparable with that emanating from anywhere in contemporary Christendom, and which would soon be widely disseminated throughout western Europe.

In these ecclesiastical centers, the monks themselves undoubtedly participated in manual work, but the vast extent of some monastic estates meant that the great bulk of the work was done by tenants who lived, with their families, on Church lands. This provided the monastic tenants with access to pastoral care, and the Church with a means of exploiting the economic potential of its estates. The consequence was that in this as yet pre-urban society many of the great ecclesiastical centers must have become essential hubs of economic activity.

Increasing secularization, wealth and lay-patronage enabled the monasteries to make an important contribution to the arts. Much of the finest metalwork of the period, including the famous Ardagh and Derrynaflan chalices, was produced under Church auspices, and the stone High Crosses still testify to the skill of their craftsmen, while the supreme masterpiece of ecclesiastical manuscript illumination is undoubtedly *The Book of Kells.*

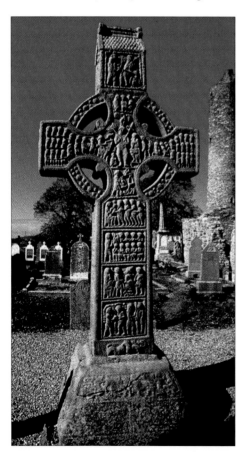

*Below: Muiredach's Cross at Monasterboice, Co. Louth, is among the most superb examples of the art form. The biblical scenes carved on the east side here include Adam and Eve, the Murder of Abel, David and Goliath, Moses striking the Rock, and the Adoration of the Kings.*

### The Golden Age

- ● *Paruchia* of Patrick (churches linked to Armagh)
- ● *Paruchia* of Colum Cille
- ● Other principal monasteries and churches
- ✝ High Crosses
- ○ Illuminated Manuscripts
- ← Saints trained in Britain
- → Missionaries abroad

St. Enda from Whithorn, early 6th century

St. Colum Cille to Iona, 563

St. Aidan to Iona and Northumbria 635

St. Fursa to East Anglia, 633

St. Finnian, from Llancarfan, c. 500

St. Máedóc from St Davids, c. 600

Irish missionaries active in Britain and Continent, from mid-6th century

Irish scholars prevalent on the Continent, from early 9th century

St. Columbanus to Gaul, 591

**ULAID**

**NORTHERN UÍ NÉILL**

**AIRGIALLA**

**CONNACHT**

**SOUTHERN UÍ NÉILL**

**LAIGIN**

**MUNSTER**

Tory
Fahan
Derry
Raphoe
Rathlin
Coleraine
Camus
Armoy
Bodoney
Ardstraw
Connor
Antrim
Ardboe
Bangor
Moville
Donaghmore
Nendrum
Tynan
Dromore
Clogher
Saul
Devenish
Armagh
Downpatrick
Inishmurray
Boho
Drumcliff
Killevy
Clones
Killala
Donaghmoyne
Achonry
Dromiskin
Louth
Fenagh
Linns
Kilmore
Monasterboice
Granard
Termonfeckin
Elphin
Kells (Iona?)
Slane
Achagower
Ardagh
Fore
Ardbraccan
Duleek
Mayo Baslick
Roscommon
Trim
Holmpatrick
Inishbofin
Inchcleraun
Dunshaughlin
Cong
Tuam
Clonard
Finglas
Swords
Glasnevin
Annaghdown
Clonmacnoise
Durrow
Clondalkin
Roscam
Tihilly
Tallaght
Clonfert
Killashee
Inís Mór
Kinnitty
Kildare
Kilmacduagh
Lorrha
Seir Kieran
Kilcullen
Kilfenora
Terryglass
Birr
Moone
Glendalough
Inishcaltra
Roscrea
Castledermot
Killaloe
Killeshin
Sletty
Leighlin
Aghade
Mungret
Ferns
Derrynaflan
Kilree
Graigue-namanagh
Cashel
Kilkeeran
Emly
Killamery
St Mullins
Ahenny
Begerin
Ardfert
Ardfinnan
Taghmon
Lismore
Inisfallen
Ardmore
Cork
Cloyne
Sceilg Mhichíil
Ross Carbery

| ft | m |
|---|---|
| 3280 | 500 |
| 1320 | 400 |
| 990 | 300 |
| 660 | 200 |
| 330 | 100 |
| 0 ft | 0 m |

0    20 km
0    20 miles

N

# Ireland and Europe

Above: *A carpet-page from the* Evangeliary 51, *an abundantly decorated book from the library of the monastery founded by St Gall, companion of St Columbanus. This volume, like others, was probably brought from Ireland, but the library also includes manuscripts written by Irish monks at St Gall.*

HAVING EARLIER witnessed the evangelizing efforts of men from Britain and mainland Europe, by the mid-6th century Ireland began to repay the debt. Although a hermit's desire to renounce home and family brought Colum Cille (Columba) to the remote Hebridean island of Iona in 563, his efforts were soon channelled into the conversion of the Picts, and his monastery, far from providing a retreat from the world, in time became the ecclesiastical capital of the Scottish kingdom of Dál Riata.

Iona monks preached the faith throughout Scotland and they later led in spreading Christianity into the Anglo-Saxon kingdom of Northumbria, their most charismatic figure being St. Aidan, the first bishop of Lindisfarne, whose activities were immortalized by Bede. Other Irish *peregrini pro Christo* ('pilgrims for Christ'), like St. Fursa, went further south to preach in East Anglia, having been granted as a monastic site the fortress of Cnobesburh (Burgh Castle, Suffolk). Fursa later turned his attentions towards France, where he and his brothers again became church builders, and he was buried in the town of Péronne in Picardy which, because of its long association with Irish clerics and pilgrims, became known as *Peronna Scottorum* ('Péronne of the Irish').

In time the trickle of Irish missionary activity on the Continent became a flood, the lead being taken by Columbanus of Bangor. He and twelve disciples are said to have left Ireland for France in 591, founding the monastery of Annegray in a disused Roman fort. Having attracted numerous followers to his austere rule, Columbanus built a new monastery at Luxeuil nearby, which became a training ground for later monastic founders. Forced out of France, Columbanus sailed up the Rhine to Lake Constance, ending up in Lombardy, where he died in his monastery of Bobbio in 615. He ranks alongside St. Benedict as the 'founder of western monasticism'.

Though Irish missionaries continued to found monasteries on the Continent into the 12th century (known as *Schottenklöster*), by the 9th century they were being followed to Europe by scholars, whose learning won them positions as masters in the imperial schools of Charlemagne and his successors. The Irishman Dicuil wrote tracts on geography, grammar and astronomy. Slightly later, at Liège, Sedulius Scottus was the leading scholar-courtier, whose works of grammar, philosophy and theology are complemented by over eighty extant Latin poems. Meanwhile, at Laon, in the palace of Charles the Bald, another group of Irish scholars gathered around Ireland's brightest star in terms of European scholasticism, Johannes Scottus Eriugena.

**Irish Churchmen and Scholars in Europe**

Route of Colum Cille to Iona, 563

Route of Columbanus to Gaul, 591

Route of Columbanus' second phase of travel

Route of Fursa to East Anglia and Gaul, 633

Route of Aidan to Northumbria, 635

Foundations of St. Columbanus and his disciples

Other Irish foundations of the 6th–8th centuries

Centres of Irish influence in the Carolingian empire

Centres of Irish influence in the 10th–12th century

Irish Benedictine 'Schottenklöster'

0    100 km
0    100 miles

N

*Faeroe Islands*

*ATLANTIC OCEAN*

Applecross △    △ Deer

*North Sea*

Iona △

△ Lindisfarne

Derry ●
Bangor ●

◇ Bangor    ◇ Mecklenburg

Bremen ◇
▽ Verden

◇ St. Davids    Cnobesburh
△ Malmesbury

▽ Münster

◇ Glastonbury

St. Omer △    ◇ Cologne
Aubigny △    ▽ Aachen    ■ Erfurt
Corbie — Cambrai △    Liège ▽
Waulsort ◇    ◇ Fulda
St. Saens △    ◇ St. Michel
Péronne ◇    ◇ Mainz    △ Würzburg
Rouen    ▽ Laon    ▽ Trier    ■ Nuremberg
△ Reims    ■ Eichstätt
St. Denis ◇    Verdun    ▽ Metz    Regensburg
Soisson    Toul ◇    △ Strasbourg    Passau ▽    Vienna
Landévennec ▽
Melk ◇    ■
Auxerre    Reichenau ◇    Göttweig
▽    Annegray    ◇ Konztanz
Noirmoutier ◇    Luxeuil ●    Rheinau ◇    St. Gall
Lure    *Rhine*
△ Mazerolles    Fontaine    *s*    *p*

*Bay of Biscay*

▽ Angoulème    *A*
Milan ▽    ▽ Verona
Pavia
◇ Bobbio    *Adriatic Sea*

*Pyrenees*

Lucca ◇    ▽ Fiesole

◇ Rome

*Mediterranean    Sea*

# The Viking Wars

WHATEVER THE underlying causes, bands of Scandinavian warriors, manning fleets of technically advanced warships, began raiding western Europe in the dying years of the 8th century. The first recorded Viking attack on Ireland took place in 795 when Norse raiders assaulted several island monasteries off Ireland's coast. Raids at first tended to be confined to the northern and western seaboards, though by 824 even Sceilg in the far southwest fell victim.

In these first four decades of their campaigns, the Vikings rarely penetrated further than twenty miles inland and were still merely sea-borne raiders based elsewhere. Periodically they plundered Irish churches, not simply because Christian targets made suitable pagan prey, but because the monasteries were important focal points of economic activity, storehouses of moveable goods inhabited by potential captives. During the next twenty years the raids intensified and the Vikings began attacking further inland. Throughout the winter of 840–841 they stayed moored on Lough Neagh and then set up a permanent *longphort* ('ship-camp') at Dublin, which in time became their chief settlement in Ireland, a secure base from which to launch extensive plunderings into the surrounding territories.

With permanent bases in Ireland, the Vikings themselves became vulnerable to attack, and from the mid-9th century, although they still threatened to overwhelm the country, one finds Irish kings successfully defeating them in battle. In the second half of the century the Vikings not only attacked Irish targets, but even took part in Irish warfare, allying with one Irish king in opposition to another. Danes competed with Norsemen for power over the Irish enclaves.

By the mid-850s great raids were on the decline, and the Vikings turned their attention further afield, to northern Britain and Iceland. Divisions within the Norse communities in Ireland, and more effective Irish opposition, led to their expulsion from Dublin in 902, and no further Irish Viking activity is recorded until 914, when Viking fleets reappeared in Waterford harbor, attacked Munster and Leinster, re-occupied Dublin and scored some notable victories against the Irish kings. For the next two decades the Dublin Vikings were very powerful and sought to reign over the kingdom of York and over the Norse of Waterford and Limerick. Thereafter their power declined, and the activities of the Dublin Norse were generally confined to the town's hinterland. By about 950 this last great phase of Viking warfare was at an end.

*Above: Round towers, though primarily bell towers, perhaps served as lookouts and refuges. This fine example at Devenish shows the entrance well above ground and easy to defend.*

*Right: Unearthed in Dublin, this drawing on a ship plank shows a man high in the rigging of a Viking ship.*

The Viking Wars

▨ Dublin Vikings active, 917–1014

▢ Viking settlement

▲ Viking encampment

★ Viking raids and battles, 795–835

★ Viking raids and battles, 836–902

→ Vikings inward

⇢ Vikings outward

*from Iona*

① Rathlin

Ailech ★   ▲ Lough Foyle
Derry ★

Maghera ★

NORTHERN UÍ NÉILL

Lough Neagh ▲   ★ Connor   ULAID
Bangor ★
Moville ★
Strangford ▲ Lough
Downpatrick ★

Clogher ★   Armagh ★★

Devenish ★

Inishmurray ★

AIRGIALLA

★

★★   ★ Carlingford ▲

★ Louth
★

★★
★★ Annagassan ▲
Monasterboice ▲

Baslick ★

CONNACHT

SOUTHERN UÍ NÉILL

Slane ★
Duleek ★   ★ Holmpatrick

Inishbofin ★

Lough Ree ▲

Clonard ★

Roscam ★

Clonmacnoise ★★   ★ Durrow   Clondalkin ▲   ▲ Dublin ②  ③

Clonfert ★   Kildare ★★   Leixlip ▲   ④

Lorrha ★

Terryglass ★   Birr ★   Kilcullen ★★   ★ Glendalough   ⑤

Iniscaltra ★   ★ Roscrea

Castledermot ★   ▲ Arklow

Leighlin ★

Limerick ▲   ★★   Ferns ★★

Cashel ★   LAIGIN

Emly ★

M U N S T E R ★

Killeedy ★   ★ Brigown   Waterford ▲   ★   ▲ Wexford

Lismore ★

Innisfallen ★

Youghal ▲

Cork ★★▲   ★ Cloyne

★★
Sceilg Mhichil

Ross Carbery ★

N

0    20 km
0    20 miles

① First Viking raid, 795

② To York, 920–940

③ To Scotland, 866–870

④ Dublin taken, 841

⑤ Danes arrive, 851 and 875

⑥ To Scotland, 918

# The Age of Brian Boru

IT WOULD BE wrong to exaggerate the ill effects of Viking attacks on the Irish Church, since the latter was already highly politicized, and monastic centers sometimes suffered as much from the depredations of rival Irish rulers as from Viking assaults. The Ostmen, as they called themselves, made many positive contributions to Irish life. They gave the country its first towns, its first coinage and more advanced naval technology. As some of their settlements grew into towns, they expanded Ireland's trading contacts and introduced its artists and craftsmen to new styles and motifs. Dublin became one of the wealthiest ports in western Europe.

The Ostmen generally governed large areas of their towns' hinterland, and in so doing displaced some minor local kingdoms. Their strength in Munster may have contributed to the decline of the reigning Eóganachta kings and to the ascendancy of the rulers of Dál Cais, who controlled the strategic lower Shannon basin. The first of their kings to attain real power was Cennétig mac Lorcáin who died as king of Thomond (north Munster) in 951, to be succeeded by his son, Mathgamain, who brought east Munster, and the Ostmen of Limerick and Waterford, under his sway. After Mathgamain's death in 976, his brother Brian Boru succeeded. He is usually regarded as the greatest of Ireland's high-kings.

*Below: Brian Boru, high-king of Ireland. This fanciful image, made many hundreds of years after his death, indicates a fond folk memory of this king who is popularly thought to have banished the Vikings from Ireland.*

Brian quickly rose to power, overshadowing his Eóganachta rivals to make himself king of all Munster. At this point he emerged as a challenge to the reigning high-king of Ireland, Máel Sechnaill mac Domnaill of the Southern Uí Néill, who in 997 acknowledged Brian as king over the southern half of Ireland (*Leth Moga*) and who finally submitted to Brian as high-king in 1002. In 1005, Brian set about asserting his dominance throughout the island, using the title 'Emperor of the Irish'. A revolt by the Leinstermen and the Ostmen of Dublin, who also raised Viking aid from Man and the Western Isles, led to Brian's great victory over them in the battle of Clontarf in 1014, at which, however, Brian himself was slain.

Brian's achievement was considerable. Early medieval Ireland did not possess a monarch whose rule was effective over the entire island, but the Uí Néill, who dominated the northern half of the island (*Leth Cuinn*), were often able to compel most, if not all, of the other province-kings to submit to them as high-king. Brian Boru, however, by making himself high-king of all Ireland, ended the Uí Néill monopoly of the title. Others in subsequent generations attempted to emulate him but none was as successful.

The Age of Brian Boru

- ✕ Successful battles
- → Successful campaigns
- → Unsuccessful campaigns
- → Naval campaigns
- → Circuit of Ireland, 1005
- → Circuit of Ireland, 1006
- LAIGIN  Kingdoms and territories

Fertas Camsa
DÁL RIATA
Ráith Mór
DÁL nARAIDE
CENÉL CONAILL
CENÉL nEÓGAIN
NORTHERN UÍ NÉILL
Assaroe
Armagh
DÁL FIATACH
Trácht Eothaile
UÍ BRIÚIN BRÉIFNE
AIRGIALLA
Dundalk
CONNACHT
CONAILLE MUIRTEMNE
Ferta Nime
SOUTHERN UÍ NÉILL
Tailtiu
Belach Dúin
Tara
Uisnech
Clontarf (1014)
Athlone
Port Dá Chaínóc
Dublin
Glenn Máma (999)
R. Shannon
Kincora
LAIGIN
Inis Cathaig (977)
DÁL CAIS
Limerick
OSRAIGE
UÍ FIDGENTE
Belach Lechta (978)
DÉISI
Waterford
Wexford
DESMUMU
Cork

1011 · 1006 · 1005 · 1007 · 1010 · 1005 · 1011 · 1004 · 983 · 993 · 1010 · 1006 · 1005 · 983 · 988 · 998 · 988 · 1004 · 1002 · 1012 · 997 · 1001 · 1000 · 1005 · 999 · 1000 · 1014 · 1013 · 1013 · 991 · 996 · 998 · 1003 · 983 · 984 · 977 · 982 · 1013 · 977 · 983 · 978 · 984 · 985 · 987 · 985

3280  500
1320  400
990   300
660   200
330   100
0 ft  0 m

N

0   20 km
0   20 miles

# Reform of the Church

FROM THE mid-11th century the Church throughout western Christendom underwent a reformation generally known as the Gregorian movement. The abuses afflicting the Church elsewhere were not absent from the Irish Church, which by then had a largely married and hereditary clergy, with individuals not in holy orders holding high office. Abbots exercised more power than bishops, and there was an absence of territorially-based dioceses and parishes. The morals of the laity were also thought in need of reform since Irish (Brehon) law allowed divorce and tolerated marriage within the Church's forbidden degrees of consanguinity.

*Above: A reliquary, the shrine of St. Patrick's bell, made around the beginning of the 12th century to house an iron bell, traditionally believed to have belonged to the Saint.*

The reforms first affected the Ostman towns of Dublin, Waterford and Limerick, which, by the early 12th century, became organized dioceses, whose bishops swore canonical obedience to the archbishop of Canterbury. More than one English primate wrote to Irish kings urging them to initiate programmes of Church reform. This began in earnest when the Munster king, Muirchertach Ua Briain, presided over two synods, that of Cashel (1101), which passed decrees forbidding simony, lay abbots, clerical marriage and incest, and that of Ráith Bressail (1111), which introduced a diocesan system for the rest of the country, dividing it into two ecclesiastical provinces, Armagh and Cashel, each with twelve dioceses reflecting local territorial boundaries. This system was later modified at the Synod of Kells-Mellifont (1152), at which Tuam and Dublin were elevated to archbishoprics. Armagh, however, held the primacy and thereby ended Canterbury's involvement in the Irish Church, a situation which pertains to this day.

Organizationally, the Church reformers were successful, though the process of dividing dioceses into parishes was protracted. The reformers also made a visual impact: Cormac's Chapel at Cashel, for example, is a notable example of the new style of Irish Romanesque architecture, and was commissioned by the king of South Munster (Desmond), Cormac MacCarthaig. Where the reforms failed were in their attempts to eradicate abuses in both the Church and society. Despite these failures, the Irish Church produced its fair share of saintly bishops, the most illustrious of whom was St. Malachy Ua Morgair, who helped end hereditary succession to the see of Armagh, and who was heavily involved in the reorganization of Irish monasticism. He converted older Irish monastic houses into convents of canons following the rule of St. Augustine, and having visited St. Bernard's abbey of Clairvaux in France, in 1142 he established a Cistercian abbey at Mellifont, County Louth. Over a dozen similar abbeys were founded in the next twenty years.

**Reform of the Church**

**Tuam** Ecclesiastical province, 1152

*Synod of Kells-Mellifont, 1152*

- ● Sees in the Province of Armagh
- ● Sees in the Province of Tuam
- ● Sees in the Province of Dublin
- ○ Sees in the Province of Cashel

- ■ Cistercian Abbeys founded by 1170
- ▲ Synods

- → Bishops of Ostman towns consecrated at Canterbury
- → Visits by Papal Legates
- → St. Malachy's itinerary

① Gilla Pátraic (1074), Donngus (1085), Samuel (1096)
② Máel Ísu of Winchester, 1096
③ Máel Muire ua Dúnáin of Meath, 1101
④ Gilla Espaic (Gilbert) of Limerick, 1111–1140
⑤ To Clairvaux and Rome, 1139
⑥ Cardinal John Paparo, 1152

Derry
Raphoe
Maghera
Connor
Bangor
Armagh
Down
Erenagh
Newry
Killala
Achonry
Louth
Kells (1152)
Mellifont (1152)
Boyle
Duleek
Mayo
Roscommon
Ardagh
Brí Meic Thaidc (1158)
Bective
Inis Pátraic (1148)
Tuam
Uisnech (1111)
Clonard
Kilbeggan
Dublin
Clane (1162)
Clonfert
Kildare
Glendalough
Kilfenora
Kilmacduagh
Roscrea
Baltinglass
Ráith Bressail (1111)
Killaloe
Kilkenny
Leighlin
Inis Cathaig
Limerick
Ibracense?
Ferns
Monasteranenagh
Emly
Cashel (1101)
Jerpoint
Ardfert
Abbeydorney
Inishlounaght
Waterford
Lismore (1166)
Fermoy
Cork
Cloyne
Ross

Armagh
Tuam
Dublin
Cashel

1124
1137
1139
1122
1142 To Mellifont
1148 To Clairvaux
St Malachy, 1140
1132
1122
1124
1127

Patricius, 1140

3280 500
1320 400
990 300
660 200
330 100
0 ft 0 m

0    20 km
0    20 miles

N

# Ireland before the Normans

BRIAN BORU'S lasting achievement was his demonstration that any province-king could make himself master of the whole island, provided his armies were strong enough. The Uí Néill, in the person of Máel Sechnaill mac Domnaill, retook the high-kingship after 1014, but with the latter's death in 1022, the title lay in abeyance. For fifty years no province-king emerged powerful enough to force his enemies into submission and make the title effective.

For most of the middle years of the 11th century, the leading contender for the high-kingship was the Leinster king, Diarmait MacMáil na mBó, who involved himself in the affairs of England and Wales, and whose power was greatly increased in 1052 when he assumed the kingship of Dublin, the first Irish king ever to do so. The practice was repeated by later claimants to the high-kingship, who sometimes appointed their intended heir king of Dublin, which in the process came to replace Tara as symbolic capital of the country.

During this twilight period Irish kingship underwent considerable changes. Wars lasted longer and were more frequent. Kings exercised more power, promulgating laws and imposing taxes, and employing an increasing variety of officials. Besides being the chosen leader of a people, kings became owners of the land, which they could grant by charter to the Church or to their vassals in return for military service, rather like feudal kings elsewhere. They invaded and conquered neighboring kingdoms, dividing them among their allies or appointing puppet rulers to govern them under their overlordship.

From 1072 until 1086, Brian Boru's grandson Tairdelbach Ua Briain claimed the high-kingship, though his son Muirchertach (1086–1119) was a more effective ruler, famous for his marriage alliances with the king of Norway and the Normans of South Wales, and a leading patron of Church reform. Subsequently, the power of the Uí Briúin (O'Briens) waned and shifted northwards. The Connacht king, Tairdelbach Ua Conchobhair (O'Connor) was probably the most effective 12th-century high-king, a prodigious builder of fortresses and bridges and master of an effective army and fleet. A declining force in his latter years, he was succeeded in 1156 by the king of the Northern Uí Néill, Muirchertach Mac Lochlainn, whose leading ally was the Leinster King, Diarmait MacMurchada (Dermot MacMurrough). Mac Lochlainn's death in 1166 led to MacMurchada's expulsion overseas by the allies of the new high-King Ruaidrí Ua Conchobhair (Rory O'Connor), and ultimately to the Anglo-Norman invasion of Ireland.

*Below: Excavations at Fishamble Street and Wood Quay in Dublin revealed the wealth and significance of pre-Norman Dublin, which by the 12th century had become the capital of Ireland in everything but name. This photograph shows a good example of a fairly typical Hiberno-Scandinavian house.*

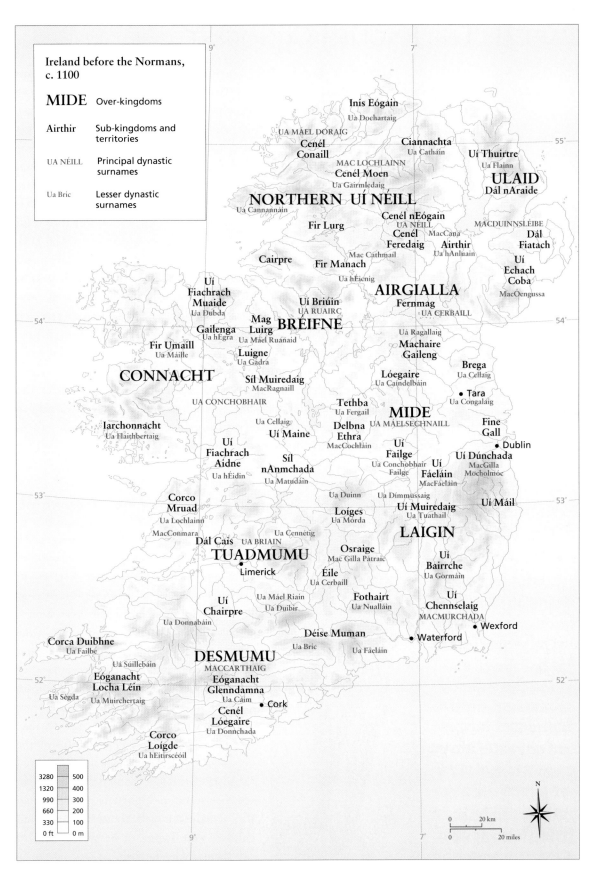

**Ireland before the Normans, c. 1100**

**MIDE**    Over-kingdoms

Airthir    Sub-kingdoms and territories

UA NÉILL    Principal dynastic surnames

Ua Bric    Lesser dynastic surnames

Inis Eógain
Ua Dochartaig

UA MÁEL DORAIG
Cenél
Conaill

Ciannachta
Ua Catháin

Uí Thuirtre
Ua Flainn

MAC LOCHLAINN
Cenél Moen
Ua Gairmledaig

ULAID
Dál nAraide

NORTHERN UÍ NÉILL
Ua Cannannáin

Cenél nEógain
UA NÉILL
Cenél
Feredaig

MacCana
Cenél
Airthir
Ua hAnluain

MACDUINNSLÉIBE
Dál
Fiatach

Fir Lurg

Mac Cathmail

Uí
Echach
Coba
MacOengussa

Cairpre

Fir Manach
Ua hÉicnig

AIRGIALLA
Fernmag
UA CERBAILL

Uí
Fiachrach
Muaide
Ua Dubda

Uí Briúin
UA RUAIRC

BRÉIFNE

Uá Ragallaig

Mag
Luirg

Machaire
Gaileng

Gailenga
Ua hEgra

Fir Umaill
Ua Máille

Ua Máel Ruanaid

Brega
Ua Cellaig

Luigne
Ua Gadra

Síl Muiredaig
MacRagnaill

Lóegaire
Ua Caindelbáin

• Tara
Ua Congalaig

CONNACHT

UA CONCHOBHAIR

Tethba
Ua Fergail

MIDE
UA MÁELSECHNAILL

Fine
Gall

Iarchonnacht
Ua Flaithbertaig

Ua Cellaig

Uí Maine

Delbna
Ethra
MacCochláin

Uí
Failge
Ua Conchobair
Failge

Uí Dúnchada
MacGilla
Mocholmóc

• Dublin

Uí
Fiachrach
Aidne
Ua hÉidin

Síl
nAnmchada
Ua Matudáin

Uí
Fáeláin
MacFáeláin

Corco
Mruad
Ua Lochlainn
MacConmara

Ua Duinn

Ua Dímmusaig

Uí Muiredaig
Ua Tuathail

Uí Máil

Loíges
Ua Mórda

Dál Cais
UA BRIAIN

Ua Cennétig

LAIGIN

TUADMUMU
• Limerick

Osraige
Mac Gilla Pátraic

Éile
Ua Cerbaill

Uí
Bairrche
Ua Gormáin

Uí
Chairpre
Ua Donnabáin

Ua Máel Riain
Ua Duibir

Fothairt
Ua Nualláin

Uí
Chennselaig
MACMURCHADA

Corca Duibhne
Ua Failbe

Déise Muman
Ua Bric

Ua Fáeláin

• Wexford

• Waterford

DESMUMU
MACCARTHAIG

Uá Súilleabáin

Eóganacht
Locha Léin
Ua Ségda   Ua Muirchertaig

Eóganacht
Glenndamna
Ua Caím

Cenél
Lóegaire
Ua Donnchada

• Cork

Corco
Loígde
Ua hEitirscéoil

3280   500
1320   400
990   300
660   200
330   100
0 ft   0 m

N

0   20 km
0   20 miles

# PART II: THE ENGLISH CONQUEST

*Brendan Smith*

THE ELEVENTH and twelfth centuries were a time of expansion throughout western Europe typified by a growth in population and an upturn in economic activity which resulted in a dramatic increase in the number and size of towns. Another consequence of this pressure of population was a colonial movement which saw lords and peasants from Europe's central zone settling in peripheral regions such as the Slav lands of eastern Germany and the Celtic lands of the British Isles. This was also an era of tremendous intellectual advance as ancient disciplines such as law, philosophy and theology came under vigorous re-examination, a process which gave rise to the earliest universities in western Europe at Paris and Bologna. Religious reform was also in the air as the Church sought to meet popular demands for higher standards among the clergy and began to emphasize a more personal approach to spirituality which stressed the individual's relationship to God. New religious orders such as the Augustinians and Cistercians offered a communal existence distant from the world, while the papacy embarked on a campaign to strengthen its authority within society as a whole. With the launching of the First Crusade, aimed at liberating Jerusalem, in 1095 by Pope Urban II, western Europe declared to the wider world a newfound energy and sense of purpose.

*Below: This illustration features Diarmait MacMurchada from a manuscript of* Topographia Hiberniae *by Giraldus Cambrensis, copied c. 1200. Diarmait was instrumental in initiating the English invasion and had a reputation as a ruthless warlord. Hence his depiction bearing the archetypal long axe borrowed by the Irish from the Vikings.*

Intimately involved in all these developments were the Normans, a people descended from Viking raiders who had settled in northwest France in the 9th century. By 1100 the Normans controlled both southern Italy and England and were helping to establish the new Crusader states in Palestine. In the short term their success rested on their martial prowess, but in the long term it was their adaptability and readiness to integrate with the peoples they conquered which secured their achievements. In England, for instance, in the years after the victory at Hastings in 1066 they formed a small ruling élite, fearful of the conquered population which surrounded them, but within a century they ceased to see themselves as foreigners and, although they remained largely French in speech and culture, were happy to be called—and to call themselves—English.

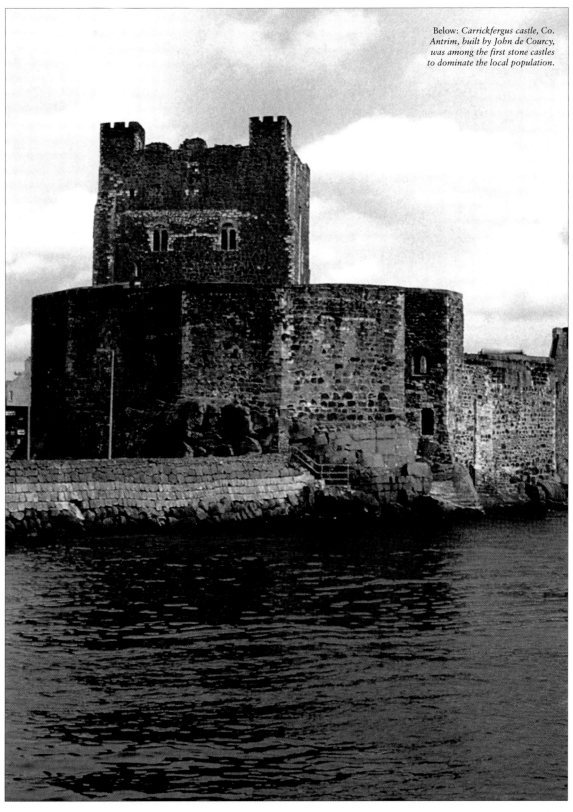

Below: *Carrickfergus castle, Co. Antrim, built by John de Courcy, was among the first stone castles to dominate the local population.*

Kings of England since 1066 had expressed occasional interest in dominating Ireland, and it was no surprise that the English should have become involved there in the 12th century. It was far from inevitable, however, that such involvement would take the form it did: that of conquest. In Scotland, Normans from England were introduced in the early 12th century under the controlling hand of the Scots king himself, and a successful blending of old and new aristocratic elements allowed Scotland to retain its position as an independent kingdom for the rest of the Middle Ages.

In Ireland, however, the existence of competing dynasties such as the Uí Néill, Uí Chonchobhair and MacMurchada on the one hand, and the failure to establish a system of succession to kingship which prevented internecine strife on the other, meant that once the English arrived in the country they were able to play different factions off against each other and to secure their own independence from the native kings.

The attitude of King Henry II was crucial in determining the character of English intervention in Ireland. He might have been reluctant to become involved, but once Strongbow had proved successful, Henry took control of the operation, thereby ensuring both that Ireland would pose no threat to England and that its rich lands would be his alone to bestow upon his favorites. Although only two kings, John and Richard II, visited Ireland in the rest of the Middle Ages, the precedent of direct royal control over Irish affairs had been set.

It soon became clear that not all the native ruling families in Ireland could be displaced and that English settlers would not come in sufficient numbers to turn the island into a 'little England'. Even the most independent Irish kings recognized the English king as their overlord, but at a local level they acknowledged the authority of a neighboring English lord only if he was strong enough to enforce their compliance. The English did not extend to the Irish their own laws, an omission which worked to the disadvantage of the native population and served to heighten ill-feeling between the two peoples. Many of the settlers assimilated culturally with their Irish neighbors over time, but this provoked harsh condemnation from the more conservative elements in colonial society, who passed

Below: *This effigy of Thomas de Cantwell in Kilfane Church, Co. Kilkenny, shows a stylized image of an Anglo-Norman knight.*

legislation, such as the Statutes of Kilkenny of 1366, to prevent the English from adopting Irish ways. Over time the settler community began to identify increasingly with Ireland and to resent the men from England who were commissioned to rule them, and the policies of the 15th century were dominated by the great settler families of Butler and FitzGerald.

The equilibrium between the two nations in Ireland could not withstand the reinvigoration of English government under Henry VII and Henry VIII, and the destruction of the ruling magnates propelled Ireland into the disastrous chaos of the 16th century.

*Below: Richard II, the last English king to visit Ireland before 1689, made two expeditions to the country, in 1394-5 and 1399. The illustration shows a meeting between Richard's representative, the Earl of Gloucester, and Diarmait MacMurchada's descendant, the reigning King of Leinster, Art MacMurchada Caomhánach. The English cavalry are depicted heavily armored, the redoubtable Art considerably less so and riding without stirrups in the usual Irish fashion.*

# The English Invasion

**DIARMAIT MacMurchada's expulsion from Ireland in 1166 set in motion a series of events which within ten years saw the kings of Ireland accept the king of England as their lord and saw vast parts of the island fall into the hands of English barons.**

MacMurchada travelled first to Bristol, with whose merchants he already had contacts, and from there made his way to France to find Henry II. After acknowledging Henry as his lord, Diarmait was given permission to recruit fighting men in England to help him recover his position in Ireland. It was among the marcher lords of south Wales that he found his first recruits.

A century of conflict with the Welsh had made these men particularly receptive to his promises of new lands waiting to be won by the sword, and their enthusiasm was sharpened by the knowledge that they did not enjoy the favor of their king. Their leader, Richard FitzGilbert, better known as Strongbow, had supported Henry's opponent, King Stephen, in the civil war which troubled England in the 1130s and 1140s, and he and his followers received no patronage from Henry after he become king in 1154.

MacMurchada returned to Ireland in 1167 and quickly re-established his position with the help of a small body of foreign knights. Strongbow arrived with a larger force in August 1170 and, with much bloodshed, he and Diarmait together took the Ostman city of Waterford. At this point Strongbow received his reward from Diarmait by marrying MacMurchada's daughter, Aoife. Dublin was taken a few weeks later, the province of Meath was invaded, and English forces raided the kingdom of Bréifne. Diarmait's death in May, 1171, without legitimate male heirs, meant that his kingdom of Leinster came into Strongbow's possession through Aoife.

Below: *The seal of Richard FitzGilbert de Clare, lord of Pembroke, alias Strongbow, the Norman marcher lord and leader of a group of Norman warrior lords based in the Welsh border lands.*

This was the signal for Henry II to intervene. He was already suspicious of Strongbow. Although he had given Strongbow permission to go to Ireland, Henry was determined to stop an independent kingdom emerging under Strongbow's rule. The king landed at Waterford with a large force in October, 1171, and received acknowledgment of his position as lord of Ireland from both the new conquerors and several of the native kings, though probably not the high-king, Ruaidrí Ua Conchobhair (Rory O'Connor). Strongbow had already offered his subjugation to the King and, having made his royal progress from his landing place to the city of Dublin, Henry II formally granted Leinster to Strongbow in return for homage and performance of military service.

At a stroke Ireland had been added to the lands of the king of England, lands which stretched from the Scottish border to the Pyrenees. Ireland had been brought into the European mainstream, but on terms which were not its own.

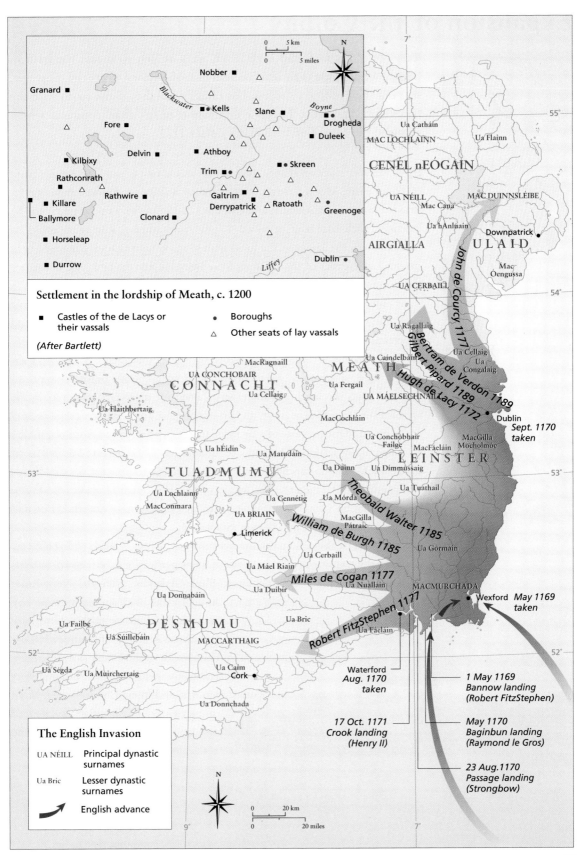

## Settlement in the lordship of Meath, c. 1200

■ Castles of the de Lacys or their vassals

● Boroughs

△ Other seats of lay vassals

*(After Bartlett)*

Nobber
Granard
Kells
Slane
Blackwater
Boyne
Fore
Drogheda
Duleek
Delvin
Athboy
Kilbixy
Trim
Skreen
Rathconrath
Rathwire
Galtrim
Killare
Derrypatrick
Ratoath
Ballymore
Clonard
Greenoge
Horseleap
Dublin
Durrow
Liffey

0  5 km
0  5 miles
N

### The English Invasion

UA NÉILL — Principal dynastic surnames

Ua Bric — Lesser dynastic surnames

→ English advance

N

0  20 km
0  20 miles

---

Ua Catháin
MAC LOCHLAINN
Ua Flainn
CENEL nEOGAIN
UA NÉILL
MAC DUINNSLÉIBE
Mac Cana
Ua hAnluain
Downpatrick
AIRGÍALLA
ULAID
Mac Óengussa
UA CERBAILL

John de Courcy 1177

Ua Ragallaig
Ua Cellaig
Bertram de Verdon 1189
Gilbert Pipard 1189
Ua Caindelbáin
Ua Congalaig
MacRagnaill
MEATH
Hugh de Lacy 1172
UA CONCHOBAIR
Ua Fergail
CONNACHT
Ua Cellaig
UA MÁELSECHNAILL
Dublin
Sept. 1170 taken
Ua Flaithbertaig
MacCochláin
Ua Conchobair Failge
MacFáeláin
MacGilla Mocholmóc
Ua hÉidin
Ua Matudáin
Ua Duinn
Ua Dímmussaig
LEINSTER
TUADMUMU
Ua Tuáthail
Ua Lochlainn
Ua Mórda
Theobald Walter 1185
MacConmara
UA BRIAIN
MacGilla Pátraic
William de Burgh 1185
Ua Cennétig
Limerick
Ua Cerbaill
Ua Górmain
Ua Máel Riain
Miles de Cogan 1177
Ua Duibir
Ua Nualláin
MACMURCHADA
Ua Donnabáin
Wexford May 1169 taken
Ua Failbé
DESMUMU
Ua Bric
Robert FitzStephen 1177
Ua Fáeláin
Uá Súillebáin
MACCARTHAIG
Uá Ségda
Ua Muirchertaig
Ua Caím
Cork
Waterford Aug. 1170 taken
1 May 1169 Bannow landing (Robert FitzStephen)
Ua Donnchada
17 Oct. 1171 Crook landing (Henry II)
May 1170 Baginbun landing (Raymond le Gros)
23 Aug. 1170 Passage landing (Strongbow)

55°
54°
53°
52°
7°
9°
7°

# Expansion of the Colony

THE CONQUERORS found it relatively easy at first to defeat the Irish in battle. What made their involvement in Irish history so crucial, however, was not their military success, but rather what they chose to do with the lands they had won. It was colonization rather than conquest which changed the course of Irish history after 1171.

Upon entering enemy territory the invaders would first construct a large mound of raised earth with a flat top surrounded by a fence, and would then build a wooden tower on its summit. This primitive castle, known as a 'motte,' could be defended with ease and provided a base from which cattle raids could be launched into the lands of the local Irish king. When the local king had been subdued, the leader of the invading force would divide the best land in the territory among his supporters, a process known as subinfeudation.

At this point the emphasis changed from military conquest to economic exploitation. The conquerors had made a long-term investment in Ireland and expected wealth in return. To achieve this they imported the agricultural system, based on the manor and on a mixture of arable and pastoral farming techniques, with which they were familiar in England. Irish peasants were not removed from the land, but there was a need for more laborers, and so the recruitment of English peasants and artisans began. Land was scarce in England at the time and the promise of new farmland and improved conditions of tenure attracted many settlers. The ports of Bristol and Chester served as points of departure for migrants who, for the most part, came from the west midlands and southwest of England. The legacy of this movement of people is seen in Ireland today in common surnames such as Bermingham, Stafford, Dowdall (Dovedale, Derbyshire) and Bruton (Somerset).

*Above: A carving representing an Anglo-Irish noblewoman, believed to be the first Countess of Ormond, in St. Mary's Church at Gowran, near Kilkenny.*

As a result of this colonial movement the landscape of much of Ireland was dramatically transformed in the space of a few generations. New towns such as Drogheda, Dundalk, Carrickfergus, Sligo, Athenry, Nenagh, New Ross, Kilkenny and Trim sprang up, their city walls and impressive castles a reminder that this was a land of conquest. In the countryside woods were cleared, arable cultivation expanded and the volume of internal and foreign trade soared. In all its history Ireland has never experienced an economic boom quite like that of the 13th century.

*Left: In many parts of Ireland the English raised mottes to defend their newly acquired territories. They were often constructed in or near an existing population site in order to exploit the maximum economic potential. This motte is at Clonard, close to the early Christian monastic settlement.*

The English hold on Ireland

English settlers

Sligo — Towns founded by the English

Ó Néill — Gaelic lordship

△ Cistercian monasteries

▽ Benedictine monasteries

● Houses of Augustinian Canons Regular

■ Stone castles

■ Mottes

Greencastle
Coleraine
Carrickfergus
Black Abbey
Grey Abbey
Ó Domhnaill
Ó Néill
MacArtáin
Inch
MacUidhir
Ó hAnluain
Down
MacMathghamhna
Dundrum
Ó Ruairc
Greencastle
Sligo
Ó Conchobhair
Ó Raghailligh
Castleroche
Carlingford
Donaghmoyne
Dundalk
Abbeylara
Fore
Tristernagh
Ardee
Drogheda
Ó Conchobhair
Mullingar
Ó Fearghail
Kilkenny West
Newtown Trim
Roscommon
Trim
Rindown
Ballyboggan
Athlone
Maynooth
Galway
Athenry
Ó Conchobair
Dublin
Failghe
Naas
Athy
Castledermot
Ó Briain
Carlow
MacMurchada
Nenagh
Kilkenny
Limerick
Graiguenamanagh
Abington
(Duiske)
Kells
Enniscorthy
Athassel
Clonmel
New Ross
Cahir
Carrick
Dunbrody
Wexford
Ballybeg
Waterford
Tralee
Tintern
Killagh
Youghal
MacCarthaigh
Tracton
Kinsale

0    20 km
0    20 miles

N

39

# Irish Resistance

RORY O'CONNOR was sufficiently powerful to force most of the important Irish kings to join him in an attack on Dublin after its capture by Strongbow, but he proved an inept military commander and his army was scattered with heavy losses. Upon the arrival of Henry II many native kings rushed to submit to him, following the advice of their bishops who saw Henry as the man to bring the Irish Church into line with the rest of Europe.

Armed resistance to the invaders did not, of course, cease completely, but the brutal treatment of those who did continue to oppose the new regime served as a powerful disincentive to others contemplating raiding the new towns and settlements or planning other forms of rebellion. Tigernán O'Rourke, king of Breifne, was treacherously slain on his way to a parley in 1172, and his head and decapitated corpse displayed at various points on the walls of Dublin after the deed.

For those kings who survived the initial English onslaught, the path of survival lay in accommodation with the new regime and in the consolidation of local power.

*Below: A galloglass (gall-óglach, 'foreign warrior'), imported from the west of Scotland. These heavily armored and well-equipped fighters effected the balance of power.*

The way of compromise, however, was not to last. Piecemeal English advance continued throughout the 13th century, and even the most compliant kings such as Feidlim O'Connor—who fought for the English in Wales in 1245—found they could not trust the king of England to keep his promises. By the 1250s a reaction had set in and in 1258 the most important native rulers challenged the English by recognizing Brian O'Neill as high-king of Ireland. Two years later O'Neill's forces were defeated by the colonists at the battle of Down, and his severed head was sent to England for public display at the Tower of London.

With O'Neill died the last attempt to revive the high-kingship of Ireland for a native claimant, but the whole episode was not without future significance. In 1259 Aed O'Connor, son of the king of Connacht, who was with Brian at Down, had married a princess from the west of Scotland who brought back with her to Ireland a force of 160 'galloglass', the fierce mercenary soldiers from the Hebrides. The subsequent employment of galloglass by other Irish kings reduced the military advantage which the English had previously enjoyed.

Irish resistance in the century after the English arrived was, generally speaking, sporadic, uncoordinated and prompted by local rather than national concerns, but it did ensure the survival of the most important native dynasties and guaranteed that the English settlers could never rest easy in Ireland.

Irish Dynasties and
English Settlement, *c.* 1300

Counties and liberties
Irish chiefdoms

*Allegiance of Irish chiefdoms*
● The King of England
● The Earl of Ulster
● The lord of Connacht
● The lord of Trim
● The lord of Thomond

*The lordship of Meath was
partitioned in 1244 into two
estates, one administered
from Trim, the other from Kells*

U l s t e r

O'Donnell

O'Neill

Carrickfergus ●

*Lough
Neagh*

MacCartan

Downpatrick
● *Down
1260*

Maguire

O'Hanlon

O'Connor
of Sligo

O'Rourke

MacMahon

O'Reilly

Louth

C o n n a c h t

O'Connor

Meath

● Kells

● Drogheda

O'Farrell

T r i m

● Trim

Meath

Galway ●

● Athenry

O'Connor
Faly

● Dublin

K i l d a r e

Dublin

53°

O'Brien

to Kildare

Thomond

Kilkenny

MacMurrough

Carlow

● Limerick

T i p p e r a r y

Kilkenny

Wexford

L i m e r i c k

● Cashel

● Kilkenny

● Wexford

K e r r y

Waterford

● Waterford

C o r k

W a t e r f o r d

MacCarthy

Cork ●

N

0    20 km

0    20 miles

41

# The Decline of English Power

**THE INABILITY of the newcomers to uproot the most powerful Irish kings and the failure of greater numbers of English colonists to settle in Ireland ensured that a complete conquest of the island could not be speedily achieved.**

However, the flame of ambition which had brought Strongbow and his kind to Ireland in 1170 continued to burn brightly, and as late as the 1230s a full-scale invasion of Connacht was launched which resulted in English colonies being established in places as remote as north Mayo.

That this impetus was not sustained was partly the consequence of many able English leaders in Ireland dying in the 1240s without leaving sons to succeed them. As a result, their estates were divided among daughters whose husbands often had no interest in Ireland and spent no time supporting or defending their holdings in the country. Violent quarrels broke out between the FitzGeralds and the de Burghs, the most important colonial families in the country, and even the suburbs of Dublin, the center of the king of England's government in Ireland, was regularly attacked, from the 1270s onwards, by the MacMurroughs of the Wicklow Mountains. The colonial parliament of 1297 painted a gloomy picture of the situation and explicitly acknowledged, for the first time, that some of the settlers had begun to abandon their own culture and instead to embrace that of the native Irish.

The weaknesses of the colonial establishment were starkly revealed when Edward Bruce, brother of Robert I, king of Scotland, invaded Ulster in 1315 and joined with O'Neill in attempting to drive out the English settlers. Despite failing to gain unanimous Irish support, Bruce was able to beat English forces on several occasions and came close to capturing Dublin itself. It was not until 1318 that the Scottish menace was finally removed with the defeat and death of Bruce at Forbart near Dundalk.

It might be said, however, that the Bruce invasion also revealed the strength of the English presence in Ireland. The settlers were united in their opposition to the Scottish invaders, despite attempts by Bruce to woo or bully them from their allegiance to the king of England.

The image they had of themselves as a conquering people chosen by God to civilize the barbaric Irish remained as strong in 1320 as it had been a century-and-a-half earlier. If anything, the decline in their fortunes in the intervening period made them even more determined to survive.

*Below: The Anglo-Irish victory at the Battle of Athenry in 1316 is commemorated in the seal of the town. The severed heads may represent the vanquished chieftains of Connacht. Five Irish kings are said to have died in this battle.*

The Bruce Invasion, 1315–18

Campaigns of 1315
Campaigns of 1316
Campaigns of 1317
Campaigns of 1318
DE BURGH    Major Family or Clan
✕    Major battle

Coleraine
Ulster
Connor 10 Sept. 1315
Larne
Carrick-fergus
O'DONNELL
O'NEILL
Moiry Pass
Louth
Down-patrick
Inishkeen    Dundalk
54°    14 Oct. 1318 Fochart
O'CONNOR
Mayo
Finnea    Meath
Granard    Slane
Connacht
Newcastle    Kells Dec. 1315
Roscommon
Trim
Lough Sewdy
DE BURGH    Meath
Athenry 10 Aug. 1316    Geashill    Casleknock
Dublin
Kildare
Kildare    Naas
FITZGERALD    Dublin
Skerries
O'BRIEN    Ardscull 26 Jan. 1316    to Kildare
Thomond    Nenagh    Castledermot
Castleconnel    Kilkenny    Carlow
Limerick    Gowran    MACMURROUGHS
Limerick    Kells    Wexford
Tipperary    Cashel    Waterford    Wexford
Kerry    Waterford
Cork
Cork
MACCARTHY

3280    500
1320    400
990    300
660    200
330    100
0 ft    0 m

0    20 km
0    20 miles

N

43

# The Gaelic Revival

THE VICTORY of the English over the Scots in 1318 did not end the problems of the colony. Ireland, which had once been an important source of revenue for the king of England, was now a heavy drain on his resources, and the natural disasters of the 14th century—famine in 1315–17 and the Black Death in 1348–49 and regularly thereafter—weakened the Irish economy still further. The problems of landlord absenteeism and feuding between nobles increased apace, and large numbers of peasants and artisans migrated back to England in the face of Irish reconquest of frontier settlements.

The greatest threat posed to the English by the Irish, however, was cultural rather than military. Beginning with the Statutes of Kilkenny of 1366, futile attempts were made legally to prohibit the English from speaking the Irish language, marrying Irish partners or fostering children with Irish families. Such a defensive attitude was a testament to the strength and appeal of Gaelic culture. In the century after 1170 this culture had been in full retreat, but by the end of the 13th century confidence had returned and the educated families of Gaelic Ireland embarked on a 300-year period of tremendous energy in the production of poetry, legal commentaries, translations of European medical treatises and works of genealogy and Irish history.

The tone of much of this cultural revival was decidedly archaic. To give but one example, ways of inaugurating Irish kings which had disappeared but 'were remembered by the old men and recorded in the old books' were revived in the early 14th century. This emphasis on continuity with the pre-invasion past could not hide the enormous changes which had occurred in Gaelic society in the meantime. The Irish had not been slow to borrow from the English in matters such as warfare, architecture and law, while Irish kingship itself had become so degraded that by the end of the Middle Ages an Irish 'king' was no longer a law-giver with a public role sanctioned by the Church, but was rather the warrior head of the local dynasty who ensured his authority by billeting his troop of galloglass on the local population. Given the power which the culture of Gaelic Ireland permitted its leaders, it is perhaps not surprising that it should have appealed so strongly to leading colonial families like the de Burghs, Butlers and FitzGeralds.

*Below: Rosserk, Co. Mayo, a Franciscan friary of the Third Order Regular, founded in the 15th century. This was a time of religious enthusiasm in Ireland. The Irish founded new monastic houses and went on pilgrimage as far afield as Santiago in Spain. Irish poets also produced quantities of religious verse of great beauty at this time.*

Gaelic culture survives
war, politics and plague

The Black Death
arrives in 1348

Plague spreads from
southeast to north and
west covering the whole
of Ireland by 1350

Ó Dálaigh    learned family and
*poetry*    particular expertise

MacCába    galloglass

Franciscan houses
founded by Irish lords
in the 15th century

MacSuibhne
**Mac an Bhaird**
*poetry*

MacSuibhne

**MacDuinnshléibhe**
*medicine*

MacSuibhne    **Ó Breisléin**
*law*

■ Donegal    MacDomhnaill

**Ó Cianáin**
*history*

**Ó hEoghusa**
*poetry*

**Ó Casaide**
*poetry*

U l s t e r

● Carrickfergus

Downpatrick ●

■ Monaghan

**Ó hUiginn**
*poetry*

Moyne ■

MacCába

L o u t h

MacDubhgaill

● Drogheda

**Ó Maoilchonaire**
*history*

**Ó Duibhgeannáin**
*history and music*

C o n n a c h t

M e a t h

Elphin ■

T

**Ó hUiginn**
*poetry*

T r i m

**MacAodhagáin**
*law*

■ Ross

MacSuibhne
■ Clonkeenkerrill

Kilconnell ■

**Ó Domhnalláin**
*poetry*

Meelick ■

Galway ●

Aran ■

M e a t h

K i l d a r e

● Dublin

D u b l i n

**MacClaincaigh**
*law*

Roscrea ■

MacSuibhne

**MacAodhagáin**
*law*

Stradbally ●

to Kildare

K i l k e n n y

MacSuibhne    C a r l o w

**Ó hIchide**
*medicine*

Quin ■

T h o m o n d

**MacCraith**
*poetry and history*

Limerick ●

● Kilkenny

Lislaughtin ■

Adare ■

T i p p e r a r y

E n n i s c o r t h y ■

L i m e r i c k

■ Galbally

New Ross ■

W e x f o r d

Wexford ●

K e r r y    MacSiothaigh

Waterford ●

W a t e r f o r d

Muckross ■

C o r k

Kilcrea ■

Cork ●

MacSuibhne

Bantry ■

Goleen    ■ Sherkin Is.

Roscommon

N

0    20 km

0    20 miles

# The Late Middle Ages

Between 1360 and 1399 the English crown devoted an unusual amount of time and money to Ireland in an effort to shore up the position of the colonists there. Edward III's son Lionel of Clarence was chief governor for five years during the 1360s, and the next king of England, Richard II, came to Ireland twice in the 1390s. Richard was deposed in 1399 and his 15th-century successors were not prepared to throw any more money at the Irish problem. Instead the great magnate families, the Butlers in Ormond and the FitzGeralds in Desmond and Kildare, were expected to represent the crown's interests and defend the settlement. These magnates had long experience of dealing with the Irish of their own districts and they had taken on many of the characteristics of their neighbors. This was not to the liking of the settlers in the towns and those who dwelt in the area between Dublin and Dundalk which by the end of the century was known as the Pale. This group wished to remain as English as possible and they sent a constant stream of complaints about the earls to London. Allowing local magnates to rule, whatever its drawbacks, did bring stability to Ireland, and the amount of new building that took place in the 15th century suggests that it was a time of modest prosperity and economic growth.

*Below: Tower houses were the most notable development in Irish secular architecture in the late Middle Ages, and were built by both Anglo-Irish and native Irish lords. This one, at Leighlinbridge, Co. Carlow, is a 16th-century device for guarding a vital crossing of the River Barrow.*

When the settlers went to England they found themselves treated as foreigners, and their feeling of resentment showed through in 1460 when they declared in the Irish parliament that they were not bound by laws passed in parliament in England unless they passed them as well. This independent stance became a major problem after the victory of Henry Tudor over Richard III at Bosworth Field in 1485 when the earl of Kildare, who had supported Richard, used the Irish parliament to forward the claim of the pretender Lambert Simnel to the English throne. In 1494 Henry VII dispatched Sir Edward Poynings to bring the settlers to heel and in a parliament held at Drogheda late that year the chief governor pushed through legislation which restated categorically the subordinate position of the Irish to the English parliament. Kildare's stranglehold on real power in Ireland survived this setback, but his actions were in future monitored more closely, and his family was finally driven into rebellion and disgrace in 1534. There was to be no Irish solution to the Irish problem as a new era of English power dawned.

Late medieval Ireland

O'Brien — Native Irish dynasties

Dalton — English names

areas obedient to England

Pale, 1488

MacSweeney
O'Doherty
MacDonnell
MacQuillan
O'Cahan
O'Neill of Clandeboye
Carrickfergus
O'Donnell
The Great O'Neill
MacCartan
Savage
O'Neill of the Fews
Downpatrick
MacMahon
Magennis
O'Rourke
O'Hanlon
Maguire
Magauran
O'Dowda
Sligo
O'Connor Sligo
MacRannell
O'Reilly
Barrett
MacDermot
Dundalk
MacCostello
O'Connor Don and Rua
O'Farrall
O'Dempsey
Drogheda
MacWilliam Burke
O'Malley
Dalton
Bermingham
Dillon
O'Flaherty
O'Kelly
Maynooth
O'Melaghlin
MacGeoghegan
Dublin
Clanricard Burke
Galway
O'Connor Faly
Earldom of Kildare
Athenry
O'Madden
MacCoghlan
O'Dempsey
O'Toole
O'More
Wicklow
O'Brien
MacGillapatrick
O'Byrne
Earldom of Ormond
MacNamara
MacMurrough
Limerick
O'Mulryan
Clanwilliam Burke
Kilkenny
O'Connor Kerry
Earldom of Desmond
FitzMaurice
Wexford
Roche Condon
Le Poer
Waterford
MacCarthy Mór
MacCarthy
Barry
Cork
MacCarthy Reagh
O'Sullivan Mór
O'Sullivan Beare
O'Mahony
O'Driscoll

3280   500
1320   400
990    300
660    200
330    100
0 ft   0 m

N

0   20 km

0   20 miles

# The Growth of Dublin

**Dublin takes its name from the Irish Duibhlinn, 'black pool,' which possibly refers to a pool on the Poddle, a tributary of the river Liffey. Duibhlinn was an ecclesiastical centre seized in 841 by Vikings who had been ravaging Ireland for the previous half-century. The alternative Irish name for the city, Á Cliath, 'the ford of the hurdles,' explains its strategic significance, as it was one of the region's most important crossing points.**

*Above: St. Patrick's Cathedral, Dublin, 1793, by James Malton. The cathedral is shown here from the southeast and it is a valuable historical document as it shows a fine example of Early Gothic architecture in Ireland before the 19th-century restorations. St. Patrick's pre-dated the English invasion, but the extant building was erected after it, and elevated to cathedral status c. 1220.*

It quickly became the main Viking military base and trading center in Ireland and its Norse, and sometimes Danish, rulers, involved themselves in raiding and military alliances in Ireland and abroad. In the first half of the 10th century members of its ruling family were also kings of York. In the course of time, though, Dublin became ever more closely integrated into Irish politics, and its Hiberno-Scandinavian rulers exercised power over its hinterland, a trace of which survives today in the area known as Fingal (*Fine Gall*, 'the territory of the foreigners').

Though a powerful military and naval force, the men of Dublin were defeated by the Munster king Brian Boru at the battle of Clontarf in 1014, and thereafter the town was largely an appanage claimed by the contenders for the elusive high-kingship of Ireland. By the time Ireland was invaded by the English in 1169, Dublin had come to replace Tara as the country's symbolic capital, and was also the single greatest concentration of economic wealth, with an extensive network of trading contacts overseas.

It fell to English arms in 1170, and when King Henry II visited the country in the following year he took the city, and what became County Dublin, into his own hands. Dublin remained the headquarters of the new English colony thereafter. Dublin Castle, which underwent many phases of fortification and expansion in the following centuries, came to represent, in both a practical and symbolic way, the seat of English government in Ireland.

In the aftermath of the English invasion Dublin enjoyed an extended period of physical expansion (including the reclamation of lands from the Liffey), and of economic development and prosperity, as exemplified by the architectural splendor of its two medieval cathedrals, and the foundation of several wealthy religious houses. By the early 14th century, however, the city had begun to decline, in common with the experience elsewhere, though in Dublin's case it lasted until the 17th century. Growth on a considerable scale only gathered pace following the Restoration in 1660, and the 18th century was arguably the most colorful in the city's history, the arts and architecture in particular finding encouragement from the wealthy society of what was now regarded as the second city of the Empire.

Dublin, 1170–1542

Oxmantown Green

St. Michan

OXMANTOWN

St. Mary's Abbey (Cistercians)

St. Saviour's Priory (Dominicans)

Liffey

St. James

Long Stone

Crane House

New Chambers

Holy Trinity Friary (Augustinians)

Guildhall

Hoggen Green

Thingmount

All Saints Priory (Augustinian Canons)

Corn Market

St. John the Baptist

St. Andrew

Old Exchequer

St. Mary de Hogges (nunnery)

Christ Church

Castle

St. George

St. Catherine

Tholsel

St. Thomas's Abbey (Augustinian Canon's)

Fair Green

St. Brigid

St. Michael Le Pole

St. Peter

St. Stephen

Thomas Court

St Sepulchre

St. Francis's Friary (Franciscans)

Donore

St. Patrick

St. Mary's Priory (Carmelites)

House of Friars of the Sack

St. Sepulchre

St. Kevin

St. Stephen's Green

### Dublin, 1170–1542

- – – Liberties borders
- Town wall with towers
- Town gates
- Cathedrals
- Parish churches
- Chapels and shrines
- Religious houses
- Hospitals
- Public buildings

*(After Clarkes)*

0   200 m
0   200 yds

N

### Dublin, c. 1800

- Built up area, c. 1685
- Built up area, c. 1800
- Notable buildings

Royal Canal

Royal Circus

CIRCULAR ROAD

Dublin Bay

Mountjoy Square

Rutland Square

Phoenix Park

Linen Hall

Lying-in Hospital

SACKVILLE ST.

Custom House

Liffey

Ringsend

Bluecoat Hospital

Barracks

SMITHFIELD

Four Courts

Parliament House

Trinity College

Grand Canal Docks

Dodder

Steevens' Hospital

Christ Church

Castle

Merrion Square

Royal Hospital

Grand Canal Harbour

St. Patrick's

St. Stephen's Green

Fitzwilliam Square

Ball's Bridge

CIRCULAR   ROAD

NEW   CIRCULAR   ROAD

OLD

Grand Canal

0   500 m
0   500 yds

N

# PART III: REFORMATION TO RESTORATION

*Colm Lennon
and
Raymond Gillespie*

BY THE END of Ireland's troubled 15th century, the English lordship of the island in practice extended over the eastern Pale region, east Munster, the towns and their hinterlands, and some scattered enclaves in the west and north. In an age of geographical expansion, Ireland became a zone of English colonial intervention and experimentation. The increasing transatlantic trade affected the thinly populated, lightly urbanized island only slowly. After the overthrow of dozens of local and regional lordships of Gaelic and Anglo-Norman origin, the political power of the English Crown became centralized in Dublin by about 1600. While the two ethnic communities of late medieval Ireland were not mutually exclusive and shared social and economic ties, their group identities were defined against English newcomers, some of whom characterized the native people pejoratively in their writings.

The genesis of the Tudors' commitment to positive policies for Ireland lay in England's increasingly complex entanglement in European diplomacy. As relations with France, the Empire and Spain deteriorated, English concern about the fragility of Ireland's defenses against continental invasion grew. The Reformation reached Ireland as part of Henry VIII's program of breaking with the papacy and chaining Church and state institutions more tightly to the monarchy. In that context the raising of Ireland in 1541 to the constitutional status of a kingdom was another assertion of royal power in the face of Roman claims that the country was a papal fief.

The kingship of Ireland was more importantly the centerpiece of a program of political and social reform designed to overhaul the Irish adminstration and to restructure the Gaelic and gaelicized lordships, bringing them into line with English norms. Originally conceived as a potential partnership of the communities within a unified constitutional framework, the putative kingdom never became a reality. In the absence of a monarch, the later Tudor viceroys attempted to persuade the native lords to accept English political relationships, common law and land tenure. But persuasion was interspersed with bouts of intimidation and with plantation ventures settling newcomers on lands to which the Crown claimed title. Resistance to English officials' increasingly forceful efforts to impose new institutions resulted in revolts in all provinces, culminating in the struggle of the Nine Years War centerd on Ulster. The breakdown of trust between the earl of Tyrone and the English authorities was symptomatic of the tense situation at the end of the century, leading to a hugely

*Below: Henry VIII of England during whose reign (1509–47) the Reformation began in Ireland and under whom Ireland was raised to the status of kingdom in 1541.*

Below: *Ireland engraved by Van den Keere, in England in 1591, published by Hondius. More accurate than the well-known Ortelius map published a year later. This is reproduced from one of only two surviving copies.*

Right: *Upon the death of Mary in 1558, Elizabeth became Queen of England. During her reign, English rule was gradually extended into all four provinces of Ireland, but the Protestant Reformation failed to win more than a small following.*

Right: *Until the early 17th century Gaelic society in many regions of Ireland remained reolatively unaffected by the policy of anglicization. Eventually, however, the power of the Gaelic chieftains and their cultural and social practices succumbed to the influence of newly-settled officials and planters.*

expensive campaign in which the Spanish monarchy intervened.

The Tudor conquest of Ireland by 1603 had come about largely as a response to rebellions throughout the island. The succeeding Stuart administration seized the opportunity for further colonization in Ulster after the pivotal event of the flight of the Earls in 1607. The central institutions of the state were in theory now effective throughout the land. The New English community comprising recently-arrived Protestant officials, planters and ecclesiastics asserted its rights to be considered the ruling class in place of the Old English élite. The members of the latter group, while not manifesting overt disloyalty, had become increasingly disenchanted with the government's political, fiscal and religious policies. For the most part they failed to respond to the state Church's lackluster evangelical campaign in support of the Reformation, instead finding their spiritual home in the European Counter-Reformation. This movement also animated key sections of the Gaelic population, some of whose leaders managed to adapt to the new political and economic realities. Most, however, lost ground to the more thrusting and entrepreneurial New English settlers.

Above: *William of Orange, later King William III of England, initially unenthusiastic about his involvement in Ireland, was drawn there by the presence of his rival James II. After defeating James at the Battle of the Boyne on July 1, 1690, he, like James, left Ireland never to return.*

The absolutist Stuart regime of the 1630s came into conflict with the parliamentary side when Ireland became enmeshed in the 1640s in the severe constitutional turbulence of the three kingdoms. The Cromwellian regime of the 1650s effected far-reaching landholding and political changes before the Restoration of the monarchy in 1660. The firmly Protestant governing establishment often faced another massive challenge to its political and religious foundations in the form of the Jacobite takeover. Once this threat was removed the response of the élite was to frame the penal legislation to defend their religion and property. After the confiscations and plantations of the previous century, the preponderance of Irish land was now owned by the new Protestant élite which presided over rapid economic growth in agriculture and manufacturing.

In town and country, the old élites had been ousted from political and economic power and distanced by the Reformation from the Crown. The Restoration represented the triumph of the new Protestant colonial class which aspired to political, social and economic ascendancy in 18th-century Ireland.

# The Protestant Reformation

THE REFORMATION was introduced into an Irish Church containing divisions similar to those in the socio-political sphere. While ecclesiastical institutions and practices among the Anglo-Irish were akin to those in much of pre-Reformation Europe, the Gaelic Church with its hereditary clerical families differed from its counterparts elsewhere. As in England, Henry VIII's legislation for royal supremacy in 1536 was the nub of a state-sponsored reform which oversaw the closure of religious houses under English jurisdiction. While Henry VIII's phase of the Reformation to 1547 was accomplished within a framework of conciliatory political reforms, the introduction thereafter of Protestant doctrines without local parliamentary sanction met with popular resistance. Consequently, Mary's restoration of Catholicism engendered little opposition from a population which included only a small coterie of native Protestants.

When Elizabeth's parliament of 1560 legislated for an Anglican state Church, the government proceeded circumspectly with the minimum of coercion. In the absence of material resources for the educating and supporting of ministers, even in the heartland of the English Pale, and with few incentives for lay conversions to Protestantism such as were available in the era of monastic dissolutions, the élite in town and countryside where the Reformation was actually preached remained aloof from state Church services. They preferred to worship in the old mode in their homes and to conserve their ecclesiastical temporalities for the later endowment of continentally-trained Catholic priests. Further alienation of the older communities from the state religion occurred as it became increasingly identified with a harsh military regime in all provinces. In the 1590s, Trinity College, later to become known as the University of Dublin, was founded as a Reformation seminary and emerged as the center of organized Protestant evangelism. Meanwhile, however, the Roman Church's Council of Trent of 1545, dominated by Italian and Spanish bishops, had met in three sessions over eighteen years and firmly established a new Catholic orthodoxy. By 1600, its 'Tridentine mission' had gained the allegiance of the majority of Ireland's Old English community. The appeal to faith and fatherland which emanated from the Ulster confederate leaders during the Nine Years War as they sought European Catholic assistance did not, however, find an echo among those loyal to the Crown. Nevertheless New English Protestants were distrustful of such 'half-subjects' and prepared to consolidate themselves into a small Protestant elect who were increasingly identifiable as the political and economic beneficiaries of the Tudor conquest.

*Below: Seminaries founded on the continent supplied Catholic priests for the Irish mission. Franciscan priest, Luke Wadding, was one of the foremost supporters of the Catholic cause in Ireland, composing spiritual texts as well as lobbying for political and financial support.*

The Protestant Reformation

Under direct royal control

Nominally under royal control but maintaining Catholic rites

Independent of royal control

Seat of Archbishopric

Boundary of Archbishopric

Diocese boundaries, c. 1570

Raphoe

Derry

Connor

Down

Bangor

ARMAGH

Armagh

Armagh

Dromore

Clogher

Kilmore

Dundalk

Killala

Achonry

Ardagh

Meath

Drogheda

Mayo

TUAM

Elphin

Annaghdown

Tuam

Tuam

Clonmacnoise

Kilmacduagh

Galway

Clonfert

Kildare

Dublin

Dublin and Glendalough

Kilfenora

DUBLIN

Leighlin

Killaloe

Ossory

Limerick

Emly

Cashel

Cashel

Ferns

Limerick

CASHEL

Wexford

Ardfert and Aghadoe

Waterford and Lismore

Waterford

Cloyne

Cork

Cork

Ross

N

0    20 km

0    20 miles

Dissolution of religious houses

by Henry VIII

by Edward VI

1 house

by Elizabeth I

several houses

by James I

55

# Elizabethan Administration

Above: *Ladies from the region of the Pale are shown here with mercenary soldiers from outside the Pale known as 'Kerns', warriors armed in the traditional Irish fashion. These illustrations were meant to contrast the civilization of the Pale with the supposed barbarism of the Gaelic west.*

THE ELIZABETHAN administration was the principal agency of the anglicization of the newly-constituted kingdom of Ireland. Its central institutions in Dublin underwent reform, although parliament met only three times during the reign. Under a succession of ambitious chief governors, the privy council was streamlined, becoming a more sophisticated and efficient executive body. The judiciary and exchequer were also overhauled, and new prerogative and ecclesiastical courts were established, those of Castle Chamber and High Commission. The huge costs of the reform program rapidly outstripped available revenues, necessitating heavier taxation of the loyal Old English. Although co-existing uneasily with newly-arrived officials, this community, residing mostly in Leinster, grew increasingly resentful, as attested by its leaders' opposition strategy in parliament over a variety of constitutional, economic and religious issues.

Some progress was made by expanding the administration into the provinces, incorporating presidency councils to foster common law, tenurial reform, abolition of overlordship and of the oppressive and arbitrary taxation known as coign and livery. The key principle was conciliation through composition, a commuting of all levies into a compound tax payable mainly to the Crown, with small residual dues to former overlords. The latter would abandon fiscal and military autonomy, and instead come to rely on the judicial and security powers of the local president. He was to rule in the manner of the lord president of Wales or the Council of the North in England. At the same time, formerly Gaelic territories became shires, leading to the insertion of sheriffs and the establishment of English-style social and landholding structures.

Whereas in Munster the presidency system broke down as a result of revolts caused by displaced Irish swordsmen, aggressive English seneschals and widespread martial law and violence, in Connacht there was attempted a comprehensive settlement known as the Composition of Connacht. This settled the landholding pattern, particularly in the south of the province, establishing an income for the presidents and conciliar courts to redress the grievances of the principal lords. But lack of consistency in English policy was most detrimental in northern Connacht and in Ulster, where peaceful reform collapsed dramatically in the 1590s.

Below: *The citizens of Dublin turn out to greet and pay homage to Sir Henry Sidney, Lord Deputy of Ireland, on his victorious return from his campaigns against the Gaelic Irish in 1575, from John Derricke's* Image of Ireland, *1581.*

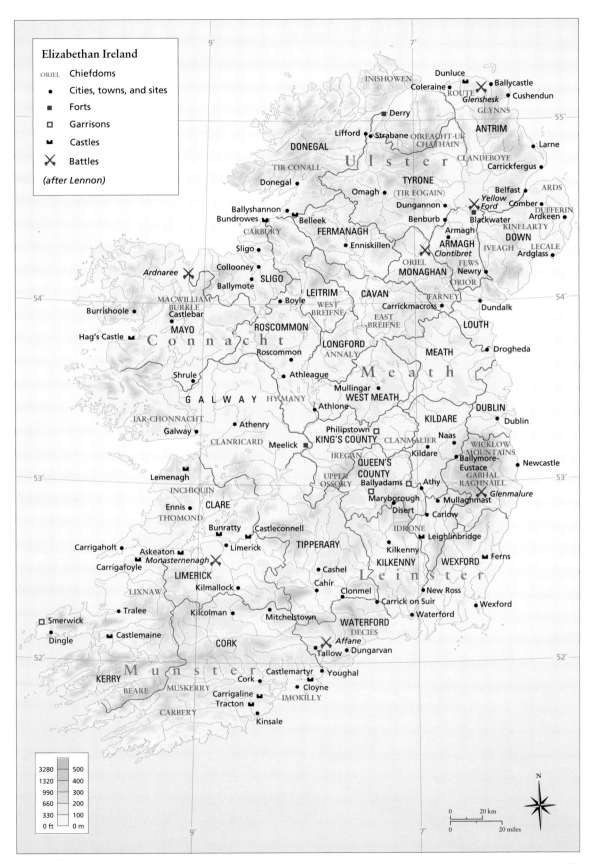

Elizabethan Ireland

ORIEL Chiefdoms
• Cities, towns, and sites
■ Forts
□ Garrisons
⌂ Castles
✕ Battles

*(after Lennon)*

# Plantation and Resistance

ALTHOUGH mooted earlier in the 16th century, plantation of Irish lands by newcomers was not actually attempted until the 1550s in Laois and Offaly. Designed principally to secure the seized estates of the rebellious O'Mores and O'Connors on the Pale borders, the settlement of soldier-farmers in what became Queen's and King's Counties did not effect peaceful agricultural and civic conditions for many years. Some natives received lands in the plantation, but others, excluded from a stake, persisted in raiding the new settlements.

Private plantations were attempted in southwest Munster and parts of Ulster in the mid-Elizabethan years. The Newry settlement by the Bagenals evolved into a sound proprietorship, but the efforts of Sir Thomas Smith in the Ards and of the Earl of Essex in Antrim failed disastrously; they were vigorously opposed by Sir Brian O'Neill of Clandeboye, whose title was overridden by the newly-arrived Englishmen. Ensuing assassinations and massacres reflected the widespread resentment stirred up. In the barony of Idrone in Leinster the Butler family and their allies revolted against the land speculator Sir Peter Carew.

The relative failure of private entrepreneurs ensured a thorough state-planned enterprise in Munster after the collapse of the Earl of Desmond's revolt. After a hasty survey of the escheated estates in five counties, the London government allotted 300,000 acres to thirty-five undertakers, principally English gentlemen, courtiers and servitors. Recipients of estates of from 4,000 to 12,000 acres, the undertakers were to foster agrarian innovation, exploit natural resources, build substantial residences, encourage crafts and attract up to ninety families to work the land.

Some undertakers became absentees, but those who stayed faced many difficulties. Some lands were not free of putative owners who claimed to be freeholders rather than tenants-at-will of the late earl, and others were burdened with debts and mortgages. Commissions were established to settle the claims of litigants, but proceedings were complex.

*Below: This map shows the Laois-Offaly region in exceptional detail as part of the movement towards its plantation, the first large-scale English settlement in Ireland since the early stages of the Anglo-Norman invasion.*

By the time of a major rebellion in 1598 and during the Nine Years War, the number of settlers was only about a third of that anticipated and the tentative roots of the fledgling colony could not withstand the avenging warbands and armies of Gaelic and Old English former landholders.

Tudor Plantations

- Plantation of Laois and Offaly, 1556
- Plantation of Desmond
- Area of Scottish settlement

# O'Neill's Rising

WHEN HUGH O'NEILL, earl of Tyrone, took the field at Clontibret as leader of the Ulster insurgent confederacy in 1595, he resolved a long-standing dilemma. Having emerged as head of the powerful O'Neill dynasty after a fractious struggle, the erstwhile protégé of the government had to choose between heading an English-style administration in Ulster, thereby alienating his Gaelic kinsfolk, or throwing in his lot with the younger provincial leaders such as Hugh Roe O'Donnell and Hugh Maguire in their campaign against the infiltration of their territories by English officials. Having committed himself to the latter course, he unveiled a professionally-trained and well-equipped army which defended the approaches to the north against advancing English armies and scored many victories, culminating in the rout of the forces of his old antagonist, Henry Bagenal, at the Battle of the Yellow Ford in 1598.

*Below: Hugh O'Neill, earl of Tyrone, was brought up among English settlers in the Irish midlands and fought on the side of the English in Munster and Ulster. Aspiring to a leadership role in central Ulster, he realized that the spread of English administration into the province represented a challenge to his position. Eventually he opted to head the confederacy of Ulster chieftains who had begun a major campaign against English garrisons and officials in Ulster in 1594. Aided by a disciplined army, he achieved many successes in the war to 1599. Thereafter the English under Mountjoy asserted their supremacy despite the landing of Spanish troops in Kinsale in 1601. The ensuing treaty of Mellifont guaranted O'Neill's headship of his clan and his title to the earldom but pressure from officials in Dublin caused him to flee Ireland in 1607.*

Now at the height of his success, O'Neill extended the war into the other provinces and renewed a quest for continental aid. As part of his campaign to enlist the support of the Old English in the Pale and in the towns, the earl issued articles demanding liberty of conscience for all the inhabitants of Ireland. Although unsuccessful in this bid, O'Neill and his allies caused the discomfiture of the earl of Essex's huge army in 1599. With the arrival of Lord Mountjoy as governor in 1600, the massive English resources committed to the quelling of the revolt began to bear fruit. By using scorched-earth tactics, suborning disaffected confederates, and establishing a garrison near Derry, Mountjoy appeared to be undermining O'Neill's campaign when a Spanish fleet containing 3,500 troops arrived at Kinsale in 1601.

After a gruelling mid-winter march by O'Neill and O'Donnell and their assault on the English armies blockading Kinsale, the fateful engagement took place on Christmas Eve, 1601, with the comprehensive defeat of the Irish allies while the Spanish remained at their base. Thereafter, O'Neill, under increasing pressure back in Ulster from Mountjoy's garrisons, eventually gave up his guerrilla war and signed a peace treaty at Mellifont in March, 1603. The terms agreed were generous, O'Neill retaining his lands and earldom but relinquishing overlordship of traditional O'Neill vassals except O'Cahan. But four years later, the earl felt so threatened by newcomers that, along with his family and retainers, and like-minded lords, he fled to the continent.

## O'Neill's Rising, 1595–1601

| | |
|---|---|
| 1600 | Landings |
| ✕ | Battles |
| —— 1598 | The marches of the Earl of Essex |
| —— 1599 | |
| ⟷ | Main passages into and out of Tyrone and Tyrconnell |
| → | Raids by O'Donnell |
| → | O'Donnell's march |
| → | O'Neill's march |
| → | Spanish arrival |
| ■ | Forts constructed by Mountjoy and Dowcra |
| | 'Planted', 1553–58 |

Lough Foyle
1600
Derry
COLERAINE
ANTRIM
Olderfleet 1598
*Ulster*
TYRCONNELL
O'Donnell
TYRONE
Mountjoy Fort
O'Neill Dungannon
Charlemont Fort
*Yellow Ford 1598*
*1597*
Ballyshannon
FERMANAGH
*Ford of the Biscuits' 1594* Maguire
*1595* Clontibret
ARMAGH DOWN
Mount Norris Newry
MONAGHAN
*Moyry Pass 1600*
SLIGO
Collooney (siege) 1599
*Curlew Mts*
CAVAN
LOUTH
Ardee
MAYO
ROSCOMMON
LONGFORD
MEATH
Drogheda
*Connacht*
WEST MEATH
*Meath*
DUBLIN
Dublin 1598
1599
1600
Galway
GALWAY
Tullamore Philipstown
KING'S COUNTY KILDARE
Maryborough
WICKLOW
Athy
Stradbally
CLARE
QUEEN'S COUNTY
Arklow
Gorey
TIPPERARY
Ballyragget
CARLOW
Limerick
Kilkenny
*Leinster*
Askeaton
Adare
LIMERICK
Cahir Castle
KILKENNY WEXFORD
Tipperary
Clonmel
Wexford
Smerwick
Dingle
WATERFORD
Waterford 1595
1596
1598
1599
CORK
Conna
KERRY *Munster*
Cork
*Dunboy Castle 1603*
Kinsale 1601
1598
*siege and battle 1601–02*
Castlehaven 1600
1601

N

0    20 km
0    20 miles

# Jacobean Plantations

ON SEPTEMBER 3, 1607 some Ulster lords, recently restored to their lands after the Nine Years War, left Ireland from Lough Swilly without royal permission. Having relinquished their allegiance to the king, James I, their lands, comprising the modern counties of Armagh, Cavan, Donegal, Fermanagh, Derry and Tyrone, were escheated by the Crown. The event was unexpected and it took some time to provide an appropriate response. In January, 1608, a plan for these counties was published involving a plantation similar to that of 16th-century Munster. Four groups were eligible for the Ulster lands: Scots and English settlers, servitors (royal officials), 'deserving' Irish and the Church. Baronies were set aside for the first three groups, who were to be granted estates ranging in size from 1,000 to 2,000 acres. The settler landlords were to introduce English and Scottish tenants onto these estates and effect improvements such as the building of towns. In 1610 County Coleraine was exempted from the scheme; the settlement there was to be carried out by a group of London livery companies and as a result the name of the county changed to Londonderry.

In the short term the impact of the plantation was much less than expected by government. Settlers did not arrive in the anticipated numbers and the social backgrounds of the landlords meant they had difficulty raising capital to improve the estates. Surveys in 1611, 1614 and 1622 provided evidence that settlers neither fulfilled their building obigations nor removed the native Irish from their lands. Much of the original settlement was destroyed by the 1641 rising.

In addition to the Ulster plantation there were smaller Jacobean settlements in counties Wexford, Longford and Leitrim, which, being mainly redistributions of land, did not require the introduction of settlers.

*Right: The town of Derry was granted to the corporations of the City of London in 1613, as part of the Jacobean plantations becoming, in the process, Londonderry. This drawing was made approximately seventy years later and shows Londonderry around 1680.*

## Irish Plantations, 1605–20

**Ulster Plantation, 1609 (*above*)**

- Subject to earlier settlement
- Scottish undertakers (estates of 2,000, 1,500 and 1,000 acres, with English or Scottish tenants exclusively)
- English undertakers (estates of 2,000, 1,500 and 1,000 acres, with English or Scottish tenants exclusively)
- Servitors and Natives (Irish tenants permitted in certain cases)
- Exceptional areas

*(after Moody and Hunter)*

**Irish Plantations (*right*)**

- Planted by 1590s
- Jacobean plantation area
- 1609  Date of plantation
- 1605  Private settlement in Antrim and Down

# The Rising of 1641

ON THE EVENING of October 22, 1641, a group of Ulstermen of native stock, under the command of Sir Phelim O'Neill, seized Charlemont Castle. They claimed not to be in rebellion against the king but took arms to protect his rights against 'evil counsellors' and even produced a forged royal commission to vindicate their action. The military campaign pushed south, arriving at Drogheda in December, 1641. This military pressure forced the Catholic Old English of the Pale to join the war, but their constitutional instinct led them to establish a representative assembly, the Confederation of Kilkenny, to negotiate a settlement with the Dublin government.

The outbreak of civil war in England in 1642 added a further complication to the Irish situation: the king, Charles I, wanted peace in Ireland so that he could use Irish troops in England. War dragged on for two years until a cessation was declared in September, 1643, to enable a peace to be negotiated between the Confederates and the Lord Lieutenant, the earl of Ormond. This proved divisive within the settler camp, and a number of military commanders appealed to the English Parliamentarians for support. The first attempt at a treaty, the Ormond peace of August, 1646, proved divisive within the Confederation, the Papal Nuncio Giovanni Rinuccini claiming there were not enough guarantees for the Catholic church. The landing of a Parliamentary force in Ireland in 1647 and plans for the second civil war in England drew together the pro-peace confederates, who negotiated a second treaty in January, 1647. After the execution of Charles I on January 30, this formed the basis of an alliance between the Confederates and the Dublin government against the power of the English Parliamentarians. Thus the Irish civil war became an extension of the English civil war, which was not concluded until 1653.

S:ʳ Phillom O Neale
Cheife Traytor of all Ireland

Left: *Sir Phelim O'Neill, leader of a group of Catholic landowners, decided to strengthen their claim to special consideration by armed revolt against the English government of Ireland.*

**The Rising of 1641**

*Situation by 1642*

Territory and towns held by the Government (all other territories and towns held by the Confederates)

*Situation by September 1643*

Territory held by the Scots

Territory and towns held by the Irish royalists

Arrival of Owen Roe O'Neill with force from Flanders

Scottish Covenanter army arrived in Ulster to support Protestant settlers

Coleraine

Doe Castle

Derry

DERRY

ANTRIM

DONEGAL

U l s t e r

Carrickfergus

Belfast

TYRONE

Dungannon
Charlemont Castle

1646 Benburb

ARMAGH

DOWN

FERMANAGH

Manor Hamilton

Enniskillen

MONAGHAN

LEITRIM

1643 Clones

SLIGO

CAVAN

Boyle

Jamestown

LOUTH

MAYO

ROSCOMMON

C o n n a c h t

LONGFORD

MEATH

Drogheda

Ardmore
Castlecoote

Roscommon

1646 Knockloffy,
Old English defeated
1647 Dungans Hill

WEST MEATH

G A L W A Y

KILDARE

DUBLIN

Galway

KING'S COUNTY

1642
Kilrush

Dublin

Loughrea

Portumna

Maryborough

WICKLOW

CLARE

QUEEN'S COUNTY

L e i n s t e r

Carlow

Bunratty

CARLOW

Limerick

TIPPERARY

Kilkenny

CARLOW

KILKENNY

LIMERICK

Cashel
1647
sacked

WEXFORD

New Ross
1643 siege

Wexford

13 Nov 1647
Knocknanuss

WATERFORD

Waterford

KERRY

M u n s t e r

Lismore

CORK

Cork

Ardmore

N

0        20 km

0        20 miles

# Cromwell's Campaigns and Administration

Above: *Oliver Cromwell, ruthless general, country gentleman, devoted father and Puritan zealot. He came to Ireland determined to stamp out military resistance to government authority, to wreak vengeance for the supposed massacres of 1641, and to convert the entire population to the Protestant faith.*

Below: *The illustration features Burntcourt (Clogheen), Co. Tipperary, a plantation mansion which had only been newly built in 1650 when it was burnt by its owner's wife to deny it to the approaching Cromwellians.*

THE EXECUTION of Charles I on January 30, 1649, united the previously divided Irish supporters of the king. The establishment of a royalist bastion close to England necessitated intervention by the Parliamentary forces. A Parliamentarian army was already in Ireland and had won a significant victory at Baggot Rath (Rathmines) in 1649. That August it was strengthened by a well supplied and trained force under the command of Oliver Cromwell, and this highly-organized and experienced army then quickly gained control of most of the country. Key east-coast walled towns, such as Drogheda in September, and Waterford in December, were taken using cannon, which had been little used in the 1640s. By May, 1650, Cromwell had left Ireland for the Scottish campaign, leaving Henry Ireton as his deputy to conclude the war, and by 1651 west-coast towns like Limerick and Galway were under Parliamentary control. The war was over by April, 1653.

The government of Ireland between 1651 and 1654 was under the control of Parliamentary commissioners who were also military officers. In 1654 one of these, Charles Fleetwood, was appointed to the civilian office of Lord Deputy, and in 1657 he was replaced by Oliver Cromwell's second son Henry. Henry Cromwell shifted the power base of the government away from the army and instead conciliated the older political élites, especially the northern Presbyterians and the Munster Protestants.

The 1650s saw a number of significant innovations: the Irish parliament was abolished and replaced by a less-than-adequate Irish representation at the Westminster parliament; the legal system was made more efficient; and educational institutions such as Trinity College, Dublin were developed to train a reliable and godly ministry.

In December, 1659, the Cromwellian regime collapsed as a result of an army coup and in May, 1660, Charles II was proclaimed king in Dublin.

## Cromwell in Ireland

| | |
|---|---|
| ✕ | Battles with dates |
| ➔ | Main route of Cromwell's campaign, August 1649–May 1650 |
| ➔ | Ireton, 1649–51 |

*Westward limits of territory held by Cromwell's forces*

- – – – December 1649
- – – – May 1650
- ▬ ▬ ▬ End 1650

### Cromwellian land confiscations, 1652–57

- ▢ Government reservations
- ▢ Land given to veterans of the Parliamentary Army and adventurers (including one mile coastal strip in Connacht)
- ▢ Additional land provided for the army
- ▢ Land reserved for transplanted Irish

# The Williamite Revolution

*Above: A medal struck to commemorate the Protestant victories, 1690–91.*

WHEN THE Catholic King James II came to the throne in 1685 there was some nervousness among Irish Protestants. James tried to reassure them with the appointment of a Protestant Lord Deputy, Lord Clarendon. Clarendon's recall in 1687 and the appointment of the earl of Tyrconnell signalled the beginning of a more pro-Catholic policy in Ireland with the Catholicization of the army and local government. While Tyrconnell wished to undo the land settlement of the 1660s, James was more cautious. The birth of a royal heir in June, 1688, caused alarm among the English political élite, who invited James's son-in-law William of Orange to take the English throne, whereupon James fled London for France.

The political situation worsened in 1688, when economic difficulties, combined with political opportunism, led to local disturbances. Memories of the 1641 rising were revived and some Protestants fled to England. Most, however, counselled caution, and in December, 1688, the closing of the gates of Derry against the army of the Jacobite earl of Antrim was regarded by many as folly. James landed in Ireland with French support in March, 1689, and summoned parliament in June. It was this parliament, with its proposal for the dismantling of the Restoration land settlement, which finally alienated James from any residual Protestant support.

William III had been reluctant to come to Ireland, but James's presence and the European implications of the French presence there obligated him. His forces arrived in Ulster in August, 1689, and William followed almost a year later. He marched south and engaged James's army at the Boyne on July 1. Following his defeat, James fled to France while William pushed his campaign west before leaving Ireland in September, 1690. The war was concluded by the Treaty of Limerick, after a siege of that city, in October, 1691.

*Right: At the end of the second siege of Limerick the Jacobites surrendered, signing the Treaty of Limerick in 1691. As a result of the surrender, many thousands of Catholic officers and soldiers left Ireland to join the armies of France. They became known as the 'wild geese' and were reinforced in the following hundred years by tens of thousands of their countrymen.*

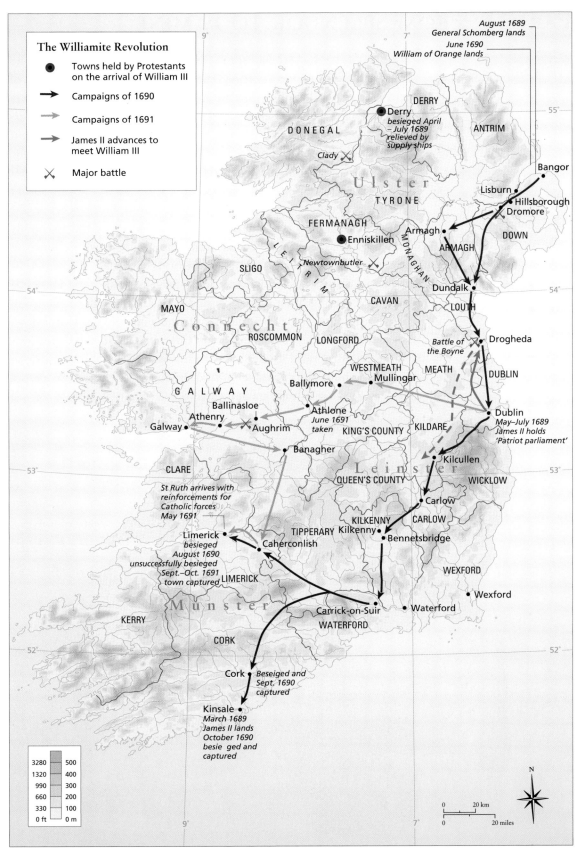

The Williamite Revolution

- ● Towns held by Protestants on the arrival of William III
- → Campaigns of 1690
- → Campaigns of 1691
- → James II advances to meet William III
- ✕ Major battle

August 1689
General Schomberg lands

June 1690
William of Orange lands

DERRY

● Derry
besieged April
– July 1689
relieved by
supply ships

DONEGAL

Clady ✕

Ulster

TYRONE

ANTRIM

Bangor

Lisburn ●

● Hillsborough
Dromore

FERMANAGH

● Enniskillen

MONAGHAN

Armagh ●

DOWN

ARMAGH

LEITRIM

Newtownbutler ✕

SLIGO

CAVAN

Dundalk ●

LOUTH

MAYO

Connacht

ROSCOMMON

LONGFORD

Battle of
the Boyne ✕

● Drogheda

WESTMEATH

MEATH

DUBLIN

Ballymore ●

Mullingar

GALWAY

Ballinasloe

● Athlone
June 1691
taken

KING'S COUNTY

KILDARE

● Dublin
May–July 1689
James II holds
'Patriot parliament'

Athenry ●

Galway ●

✕ Aughrim

● Banagher

CLARE

St Ruth arrives with
reinforcements for
Catholic forces
May 1691

Leinster

QUEEN'S COUNTY

● Kilcullen

WICKLOW

Limerick ●
besieged
August 1690
unsuccessfully besieged
Sept.–Oct. 1691
town captured

Caherconlish ●

TIPPERARY

KILKENNY

Kilkenny ●

● Carlow

CARLOW

● Bennetsbridge

WEXFORD

LIMERICK

Munster

KERRY

CORK

Carrick-on-Suir ●

● Waterford

● Wexford

WATERFORD

Cork ●  Beseiged and
Sept. 1690
captured

Kinsale ●
March 1689
James II lands
October 1690
besie ged and
captured

| 3280 | 500 |
| 1320 | 400 |
| 990 | 300 |
| 660 | 200 |
| 330 | 100 |
| 0 ft | 0 m |

N

0    20 km

0    20 miles

# PART IV: FROM SPLENDOR TO FAMINE

*James Kelly*

COMPARED WITH the 16th and 17th centuries, the 18th century in Ireland appears quiescent and uneventful. There was, it is true, no outbreak of serious religico-political conflict until the 1790s, but both Irish society and politics were less consensual and politics more eventful than the visible absence of civil discord suggests. There is some disagreement between historians as to how we can best interpret Irish society during this period. In his provocative study of 'the making of Protestant Ireland,' Sean Connolly has shown how comparable 18th-century Ireland was to other 'ancien régime' societies. From this perspective, the tensions and conflicts that can be identified arose out of the essentially hierarchical character of its social organization, and mirror equivalent phenomena in Britain and on the continent. If this was all, it would be possible to dispense with the traditional perception that the most formative influence on Irish politics during the Georgian era was its colonial subordination to Britain and that the most consequential feature of Irish society was that the preeminently Catholic Gaelic population was ruled by an introduced Anglophone landowning élite, but the two views need not be mutually exclusive. Indeed, Irish history during this period makes more sense if both are appealed to.

Below: *In all its glittering finery, a state ball held in Dublin Castle, painted by William van der Hagen in 1731.*

There is certainly much to sustain a colonial interpretation from a political per-spective. It is significant, for example, that the head of the Irish administration (the Lord Lieutenant) was appointed by the Crown on the recommendation of the British government, and was seldom entrusted to anybody other than Englishmen. This led to the practice for much of the 18th century of lords lieu-tenant not residing permanently in Ireland for the duration of their posting but, significantly, did not result in a dramatic transfer of power to Irish-born offi-cials. Indeed, successive governments insured against this by determining that the most important offices of state were filled by Englishmen.

Allied with this, the Crown could avail of Poynings' Law (1494), which gave the English (from 1707, the British) Privy Council the power to respite and to amend all legislation emanating from the Irish parliament, and to the Declaratory Act (1719), which made the House of Lords at Westminster the final court of legal appeal in Irish law cases and gave the British parliament the power to make law for Ireland.

If this combination of practices and powers suggest that Ireland's position within the British empire was irrevocably colonial, the emergence of a persua-sive Irish Protestant critique of the dependent position to which their kingdom was consigned, defined influentially by J. G. Simms as *colonial nationalism*,

Below: *The Dublin Volunteers saluting the Statue of William III on College Green, 4 November 1779.*

would seem to indicate that this was how Irish Protestants saw it as well. In fact Simms' 'colonial nationalism' can be interpreted equally plausibly as an Irish manifestation of the Europeanwide phenomenon of civic humanism or 'patriotism' because, like its European parallels, the Irish phenomenon placed similar emphasis on political virtue and domestic economic improvement.

More significantly, from the moment it was given political coherency by William Molyneux in his seminal tract *The case of Ireland's being Bound by Acts of Parliament in England Stated* in the late 1690s, equality with Britain was the political *raison d'être* of Irish Protestant Patriots. This is why Molyneux could describe a legislative union as 'an happiness we can hardly hope for,' and why the Irish parliament responded to the Anglo-Scottish union of 1707 by appealing to Queen Anne to expedite a similar arrangement with respect to Ireland. However, because neither Queen Anne nor her ministers who, like most English politicians and opinion makers, regarded and treated Ireland as a colony, could perceive any advantage in such an arrangement as long as the Irish parliament continued to vote the revenue needed to fund the Irish army establishment and to pay for the administration of the kingdom, the address was ignored.

This did not please Irish Protestants, and they responded to this and to other manifestations of British unwillingness to acknowledge their equal status under the Crown by asserting their right to govern themselves on the same terms as Englishmen and the equality of the kingdom of Ireland with that of Britain. This is why when, after many decades of pursuing this cause, the Patriots were able to take advantage of the government's difficulties in the American colonies to compel them to repeal the bulk of the laws confining Ireland's freedom to trade in 1779–80 and to accede to the removal or modification of the restrictions on the legislative authority of the Irish parliament, they did not seek to emulate the Americans and achieve independence. Quite the contrary; they did not want separation, just the power to govern. Indeed, so strong was their fear of doing anything that would endanger the Anglo-Irish connection, upon which they realized the security of their ascendant position in Ireland rested, that they made no attempt to challenge the British government's right to nominate the head of the Irish administration and declined an opportunity to reform the Irish legislature to make it more representative of the Protestant population at large.

As this, and the decision of the Irish parliament in 1800 to vote itself out of existence bears witness, a large percentage (probably a majority during the bulk of this era) of Irish Protestants preferred the security of a close (and, if necessary, a dependent) relationship with Britain, because fundamentally the maintenance of what they then termed their ascendancy *vis à vis* the Catholic population was their priority and they perceived its perpetuation as dependent upon the retention of an intimate Anglo-Irish nexus. This is why it is not a coincidence that the decade which saw the advancement by the United Irishmen of the virtues of a republic culminated with the decision of the Irish ruling élite to opt to govern Ireland from Westminster rather than to continue to do so from College Green.

If this conforms to a colonial pattern, there is also much to sustain Connolly's view that Ireland was an *ancien régime* society. Thus, like most European countries, land was owned by a relatively small number of large landowners and worked by tenant occupiers, who were expected to defer to their social superiors and to assent to their social, economic and political dominance locally as well as nationally. Moreover, as was the case elsewhere, the members of this landed élite were convinced that they were the natural repository of government on the island because only they were equipped economically and intellectually to rule.

The situation in Ireland was complicated by the fact that the religion of the bulk of this élite (the Church of Ireland) differed from that of the majority of the population, but the élite secured itself in this respect by defining itself as the political nation and by implementing a corps of discriminatory legislation (the Penal Laws) which secured them economically, socially and politically against the Catholic majority. For most of the 18th century, indeed, their rule was unchallenged, and the fact that the Irish economy embarked on one of its most sustained periods of growth once it had negotiated poor harvests, famine and

*Above: Ireland's ruling élite aristocracy and country landowners embraced the 'Georgian' style with enthusiasm. Many great houses were built or rebuilt. Shown here is Caledon, seat of the Earl of Caledon, Co.Tyrone, completed in 1794.*

epidemic disease between 1725 and 1745 seemed to suggest it was advantageous to the country.

The economic, and consequent demographic, expansion that was a feature of the second half of the 18th century was not due simply to the guidance of the Protestant élite. But the enthusiasm for improvement manifested by its members, the contributions they made to the success of the linen industry and to advances in internal navigation, to urban development, the enhancement of the road network, land enclosure, demesne development and 'big house' construction all attest to its weighty imprint.

This activity and the rise in population from *c.* 2 million in 1750 to *c.* 4.5 million in 1790 were the most tangible manifestations of the greater prosperity of the Irish economy, but they did not prove equally beneficial to all. Many outside the élite were gravely discommoded by the commercial forces that were released, and this led to a marked upsurge in agrarian unrest from the 1760s. This was essentially conservative in thrust for several decades, but sectarian passions lay just beneath the surface, and when they fused with the reformist and revolutionary doctrines emanating from Britain and France in the 1790s, they facilitated the dissemination of republican ideas, which in the second half of the 1790s posed the confessional *ancien régime* state and colonial Anglo-Irish nexus a formidable challenge that climaxed with the explicitly separatist intent of those who rose in rebellion in 1798.

This was overcome, but the price the Anglo-Irish élite had to pay was high because the Act of Union which followed changed the context within which Irish politics were conducted. If most Irish Protestants had no difficulty accepting this, many Catholics too were content. They believed the abolition of the Irish parliament would pave the way for the repeal of the last major penal disability— the prohibition on Catholics sitting in parliament. However, the united parliament proved less than accommodating.

As a consequence, a more broad-based and assertive Catholic leadership, spearheaded by Daniel O'Connell's Catholic Association, emerged in the 1820s to advance the issue. They eventually obliged ministers to give way in the course of which they shattered the *ancien régime* mould forever. Schooled in the emerging precepts of democracy by the Association, O'Connell subsequently took up the repeal of the Act of Union in a vain attempt to restore domestic government to Ireland. He was unable to make much progress on the matter, but having transformed Irish politics by creating an active Catholic political interest, he also gave parliamentary politics the key feature of its political agenda for the rest of the century.

At the same time, the priority of the Catholic masses was fixed on the more elemental matter of survival. Following the ending of the Napoleonic wars, the Irish economy embarked on a period of uncertainty. Agricultural exports grew, but the economy was unable to offer security against famine to the rising number of poor and vulnerable among a population which neared 7 million in 1821. Industrialization would have reduced their vulnerability, but the failure of the cotton industry and the mechanization of linen manufacture indicated its limited potential, so that when the country's main staple foodstuff—the potato—was seriously damaged in the late 1840s, a crisis of cataclysmic proportions ensued which changed both Irish society and politics irrevocably.

*Below: Lord Grandison, a landowner concerned with improving his estates, created carefully designed housing on his estates. Below is an illustration showing a range of houses to be assigned to tradesmen on his Waterford property.*

# The Penal Laws

As a consequence of the military triumph of the Williamites in 1690–91, political authority in Ireland was restored to the Protestant interest, from whom it had been removed during the reign of James II. Convinced by their experiences, and their cultivation of an exaggeratedly baleful memory of the 1641 'massacres,' that the Catholics were irrevocably committed to their destruction, many Protestants shared the conclusion of Edward Wetenhall, Church of Ireland bishop of Limerick, that in time there would be a repeat of the events of the 1640s and 1680s if immediate steps were not taken to weaken the Catholic interest. Such conclusions were encouraged by reports in the 1690s that Irish Catholic emigrés were actively pursuing schemes to bring about another French invasion, and by the visible Jacobitism of Catholic priests and ecclesiastics. Indeed, Wetenhall and those of like mind believed that the ratification and enforcement of anti-Catholic law was a matter not of vengeance but of survival.

| Percentage of households Catholic – 1732 | |
| --- | --- |
| Leinster | 79% |
| Ulster | 38% |
| Munster | 89% |
| Connacht | 91% |
| Nationally | 73% |

Anti-Catholic legislation would serve both to secure the political, economic and social ascendancy of Protestants in Ireland and to increase their number by inducing Catholics to embrace the Protestant religion. Many influential figures in the corridors of power were not convinced of the wisdom of such a course. They sought to honor the spirit of the Treaty of Limerick which offered Catholics an ambiguous promise of toleration, and ensured that no specifically anti-Catholic legislation of Irish origin was ratified in the early 1690s. However, Catholics were precluded by the adoption in 1692 of an English oath from sitting in parliament, and as Dublin Castle struggled in the mid-1690s to win the support of sufficient MPs to ensure the smooth administration of the country, they were obliged to bow to demands for laws to restrict the freedoms of Catholics and the Catholic Church. Thus in 1697, the first of a number of measures, culminating in the 1703 act for registering clergy, was ratified with the purpose of depriving Catholics of ecclesiastical leadership and of limiting the number of clergy in the country. In the years that followed, restrictions were also imposed on the freedom of Catholics to educate their children, to carry arms, inherit, own, lease and work land, to trade and employ, to enter the major professions and, finally in 1728, to vote.

Having already suffered the loss of their lands and traditional leaders to war and to emigration, the Catholics were ill-prepared to resist this legislation. The Penal Laws, as they became known, were not devised systematically to weaken Catholics in every area of life, but they did serve to exclude them from the political process until the 1790s and to hinder their economic advancement.

The Penal Laws were less effective in the religious sphere. The restrictions imposed on the Catholic Church caused serious problems nationally for a number of decades, particularly at times of Jacobite activity, and provided antipathetic landlords with plenty of opportunities to obstruct its mission. But the Church never experienced the shortage of priests or the virulent repression it endured in the early 1650s, and from the mid-1720s it enjoyed a sufficiency of clergy and the freedom to operate competently, if not without difficulty or fear.

**The Penal Laws**

*Percentage of land in Catholic ownership, 1703:*

- 25 or more
- 11 to 24
- 10 or less

(19) Number of Catholic gentlemen licensed to bear arms, 1704

45 Registered Catholic clergy per county, 1704

DERRY
14

ANTRIM
18

DONEGAL
(1)
21

Ulster

DOWN
(2)
30

TYRONE
27

FERMANAGH
13

ARMAGH
19

MONAGHAN
17

SLIGO
39

LEITRIM
25

CAVAN
30

LOUTH
(2)
16

MAYO
(4) 51

ROSCOMMON
(1)
49

LONGFORD
(1)
18

Connacht

WESTMEATH
(10)
35

MEATH
(9)
57

DUBLIN
(34)
70

GALWAY
(9)
95

Leinster

KING'S CO.
(2)
20

QUEEN'S CO.
(2)
15

KILDARE
(5)
30

WICKLOW
13

CLARE
(3) 45

TIPPERARY
(8)
62

KILKENNY
(4)
30

CARLOW
(3)
14

WEXFORD
(4)
34

LIMERICK
(2) 59

KERRY
36

CORK
(3) 60

WATERFORD
(4) 27

Munster

Lough Neagh

0    20 km

0    20 miles

N

77

# The Georgian Economy

THE INFLUENCE of the Protestant interest in Ireland peaked in the 18th century. Politically, this can be pinpointed to the sixty-five years between 1728 and 1793 when, as well as their exclusion from parliament, Catholics did not possess the franchise. These are the decades commonly regarded as the high point of Protestant ascendancy, though this term is problematic because of its use by conservative Protestants from the 1780s to justify their undiluted predominance. There was a widespread Protestant perception, articulated in 1781 by Henry Flood, that they were 'the people of Ireland,' an exclusive vision, but one softened by their commitment to the island's economic development. This enthusiasm for improvement took many forms, one of the most important of which was the establishment in 1711 of the Linen Board. This body enforced quality controls on the production and sale of exported linens, establishing the industry as the country's leading currency-earner and resulting in the emergence of Ulster as its wealthiest and most populous province.

Efforts by landowners to establish linen operations elsewhere in the country proved less successful, but other initiatives continued. Indeed, at both local and national levels the ruling élite assiduously sought to remold both the rural and urban landscapes in the Anglican image they held dear. Some of their schemes, like the proliferation of Palladian and neoclassical residences and carefully landscaped demesnes, were primarily self-serving, but they did facilitate the dissemination of new techniques in construction and internal design and employed craftsmen from a multiplicity of trades. Other improvements such as the creation of a road network, widely regarded in the late 18th century as one of the best in Europe, the enhancement of internal navigation through the construction of canals and the drainage of rivers, and the creation of a network of estate villages were less personally motivated, though they well fitted the vision of a tidy landscape. Urban development on a substantial scale was fostered in cities like Dublin, Limerick, Cork and Waterford. In Dublin the crowded warrens of medieval streets were swept away by the Wide Streets Commissioners, and a lattice of straight, broad thoroughfares linking the elegant Georgian streets and squares on the north and south sides of the River Liffey was put in their place. Combined with fine new public buildings including a new parliament, customs house, city exchange and courts, they transformed the city into one of the most attractive of the period, and a crowning symbol of the vision and achievement of the Protestant interest in Ireland.

*Below: Medieval buildings were swept aside to make room for Georgian ideas of elegance in buildings and landscapes. Here the home of the Duke of Abercorn sits amongst its well-groomed 'landscape'.*

## The Georgian economy

—— Main roads

—— Secondary roads

—— Canals

*Value of linen sent to market, per county, 1771:*

◯ Over £100,000 (main region)

◯ £40,000 to £100,000 (peripheral region)

◼ Main brown linen market, 1783

➤ Main export, 1780

*Linen*

Coalisland Canal

Coleraine
Ballymoney
Derry
ANTRIM
Lifford
DERRY
Ballymena
Strabane
DONEGAL
TYRONE
Belfast
Stewartstown
Lurgan
Lisburn
Dungannon
Portadown
Augher
Armagh
DOWN
Sligo
Enniskillen
FERMANAGH
ARMAGH
Newry
Newry Canal
Sligo
MONAGHAN
Linen
SLIGO
Dundalk
Boyle
LEITRIM
CAVAN
LOUTH
MAYO
Castlebar
ROSCOMMON
LONGFORD
Linen
Longford
Drogheda
Roscommon
Royal Canal
Mullingar
MEATH
Beef
Pork
Butter
WESTMEATH
Athlone
DUBLIN
Ballinasloe
KILDARE
Dublin
GALWAY
KING'S CO.
Grand Canal
Galway
Barrow
Line
Naas
WICKLOW
Wicklow
QUEEN'S CO.
Ennis
CLARE
CARLOW
WEXFORD
Beef
Pork
Limerick
TIPPERARY
KILKENNY
Enniscorthy
Cashell
Callan
LIMERICK
New Ross
Clonmell
Wexford
KERRY
Waterford
Tralee
WATERFORD
Killarney
Dungarvan
Beef
Pork
Butter
CORK
Cork
Lismore Canal
Beef
Pork
Butter
Lombardstown Canal

| | |
|---|---|
| 3280 | 500 |
| 1320 | 400 |
| 990 | 300 |
| 660 | 200 |
| 330 | 100 |
| 0 ft | 0 m |

N

0   20 km

0   20 miles

# The Government of Ireland, 1692–1785

LONDON'S decision in the early 1690s to entrust the responsibility of raising revenue and making law to an Irish parliament determined the character of 18th-century government. Like its British counterpart, the Irish parliament had two chambers. The House of Lords consisted of a fluctuating number of temporal and a fixed number of religious peers, while the House of Commons comprised 300 representatives chosen from 150 constituencies of varying antiquity and franchise. It was an exclusively Protestant assembly because of the Irish parliament's decision to follow the Westminster precedent requiring all members to swear an oath of adjuration. The parliament sat for approximately six months every two years between 1692 and 1784, and annually thereafter, affording Irish Protestants a central role in the administration of their kingdom. The parliament's powers, however, were severely circumscribed by Poynings' Law and the Declaratory Act, and by the fact that the Irish executive at Dublin Castle was not responsible to parliament and that its head, the Lord Lieutenant, was a nominee of the British government.

Despite these constraints, the members of the Irish parliament, particularly the Commons, sought to play an active part in the administration of the kingdom. Because of this, and the disinclination of successive lords lieutenant to keep tight personal control of the levers of power by residing in Ireland throughout the terms of their appointment, the day-to-day duties of administration were shared between English-born officeholders and able Irish politicians (commonly termed 'undertakers') who agreed, in return for preferment and influence, to manage the parliament on the Lord Lieutenant's behalf.

This arrangement worked satisfactorily from its inception in 1695 until the 1750s, when a disruptive power struggle between Henry Boyle and John Ponsonby prompted a reassessment, and it was decided, eventually, that lords lieutenant should reside in Ireland for the duration of their appointment.

The decision of Lord Townshend to become a residential lord lieutenant in the late 1760s contributed to the emergence of the 'Patriots,' whose object was to dilute the legal constraints on the legislative authority of the Irish parliament and to secure the right to free trade. Detachments of Volunteers —loosely organized associations of armed men whose primary purpose was to support the regular army— became politicized, and their extra-parliamentary lobbying was decisive in securing both free trade (1780) and legislative independence (1782). However, their attempts to secure direct admission to the political process by reforming the electoral system were thwarted by the small and unrepresentative élite that controlled most of the parliamentary constituencies.

*Above: Silver-gilt mace, the symbol of authority of the old Irish House of Lords. This elegant silver work was made in Dublin around 1760.*

*Left: This medallion was presented to the 1st Ulster Regiment of Irish Volunteers and would be worn by the best shot in the regiment 'so long as he shall maintain this superior skill at the target'.*

FIRST ULSTER BEST
The coat of THE
EARL OF CHARLMONT
The best Shot to wear this
PRIZE MEDAL
so long as he shall maintain
his superior skill at the
TARGET

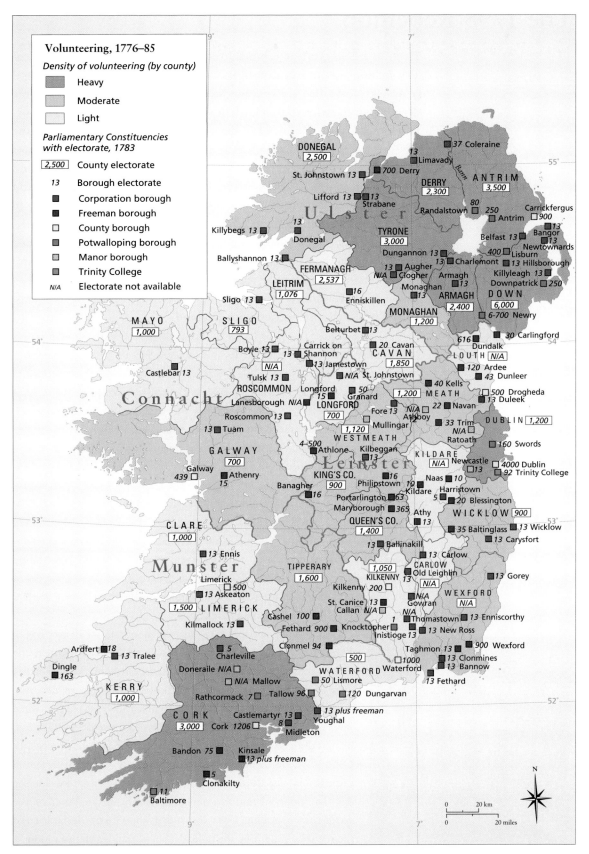

## Volunteering, 1776–85

*Density of volunteering (by county)*

- Heavy
- Moderate
- Light

*Parliamentary Constituencies with electorate, 1783*

- 2,500 — County electorate
- 13 — Borough electorate
- ■ Corporation borough
- ■ Freeman borough
- □ County borough
- ■ Potwalloping borough
- □ Manor borough
- ■ Trinity College
- N/A — Electorate not available

DONEGAL 2,500

37 Coleraine
13 Limavady
700 Derry
St. Johnstown 13
ANTRIM 3,500
DERRY 2,300
Lifford 13 ■ 13 Strabane
Randalstown 80
250 Antrim
Carrickfergus
900
Killybegs 13 ■ 13
Donegal
Belfast 13 ■ 13 Bangor
13 Newtownards
Dungannon 13
400 Lisburn
TYRONE 3,000
13 Charlemont 13 Hillsborough
Ballyshannon 13 ■
13 Augher
Killyleagh 13
FERMANAGH 2,537
N/A Clogher
Armagh 13
Downpatrick ■ 250
LEITRIM 1,076
16 Enniskillen
Monaghan 13
DOWN 6,000
Sligo 13 ■
ARMAGH 2,400
6-700 Newry
MONAGHAN 1,200
Belturbet ■ 13
616
30 Carlingford
MAYO 1,000
SLIGO 793
20 Cavan
CAVAN 1,850
Dundalk N/A
LOUTH N/A
Boyle 13 ■ 13 ■ Carrick on Shannon
120 Ardee
Castlebar 13
Tulsk 13 ■
13 Jamestown
N/A St. Johnstown
43 Dunleer
Connacht
N/A
40 Kells
ROSCOMMON
Longford 50
13 Duleek
500 Drogheda
Lanesborough N/A
15 Granard
MEATH 1,200
Roscommon 13 ■
LONGFORD 700
Fore 13
22 Navan
DUBLIN 1,200
13 ■ Tuam
Mullingar
N/A Athboy
33 Trim
4-500
1,120
N/A Ratoath
GALWAY 700
Athlone 13
WESTMEATH
Kilbeggan
KILDARE N/A
160 Swords
Leinster
Newcastle
4000 Dublin
Galway 439 □
Athenry
KING'S CO. 900
16
Naas 10
13
92 Trinity College
15
Philipstown 19
Kildare
Harristown
Banagher
16
Portarlington 63
5
20 Blessington
Maryborough 365
Athy
WICKLOW 900
QUEEN'S CO. 1,400
13
35 Baltinglass 13 Wicklow
13 Carlow
13 Carysfort
13 ■ Ballinakill
CLARE 1,000
13 Ennis
TIPPERARY 1,600
1,050
Old Leighlin
13 Gorey
Munster
Limerick 500
KILKENNY N/A
13
Kilkenny 200
CARLOW
WEXFORD N/A
13 Askeaton
St. Canice 13
Gowran N/A
Callan N/A
1,500 LIMERICK
Cashel 100
1
13 Enniscorthy
Kilmallock 13
Fethard 900
Knocktopher
Thomastown
13 New Ross
Clonmel 94
Inistioge 13
Ardfert 18
Taghmon 13
900 Wexford
13 Tralee
5 Charleville
13 Clonmines
Dingle 163
Doneraile N/A
500
13 Bannan
N/A Mallow
WATERFORD Waterford 1000
KERRY 1,000
Rathcormack 7
Tallow 96
50 Lismore
13 Fethard
CORK 3,000
Castlemartyr 13
120 Dungarvan
13 plus freeman
Cork 1206 □
8
Youghal
Midleton
Bandon 75
Kinsale 13 plus freeman
5 Clonakilty
11 Baltimore

N

0    20 km
0    20 miles

# The 1798 Rebellion

THOUGH THE impression is often given, it is not true to say that 18th-century Ireland was peaceful until its last decade. The readiness of rural protesters to swathe themselves in Jacobite white suggests that they were already politicized, and that ancient sectarian loyalties remained strong. This conclusion is reinforced by the emergence in County Armagh in the 1780s of the Catholic Defenders to resist disarming raids by Protestant Peep O'Day Boys. At the same time, elements within the Protestant and Presbyterian middle classes offered an alternative non-sectarian vision and they were encouraged by the outbreak of the French Revolution in 1789 to launch a campaign to reform the representative system to satisfy their wishes. The organization they established in 1791 to spearhead their campaign took the name United Irishmen from Wolfe Tone's inspirational claim that it would only be possible to overcome the country's problems if Catholic, Protestant and Dissenter came together and Ireland broke the connection with England.

To begin with, the United Irishmen devoted their energies to the cause of reforming the representative system. Catholics were indeed conceded the franchise in 1793, but the fact that it was implemented on the insistence of London indicates how unimportant was the United Irishmen's efforts. The conservative-dominated parliament embarked at the same time on a strategy to weaken its radical critics by replacing the Volunteers with a Castle-controlled militia. However, instead of destroying the movement, this strategy allowed revolutionary separatists within the organization to capitalize on the growing discontent throughout the country with the government's uncompromising policies and the premature recall, in 1795, of the liberal Lord Lieutenant, Earl Fitzwilliam. The United Irishmen then formed an alliance with the Catholic Defenders, and the movement was reconstituted along revolutionary lines. They were remarkably successful in recruiting members and in disseminating their message and, encouraged by the success of Wolfe Tone's diplomatic efforts to enlist the support of the French, were hopeful that a successful rebellion could be orchestrated.

*Below: Members of the Society of United Irishmen take an oath to rise against English rule.*

A large-scale invasion force attempted to land off Bantry Bay in 1796; if the fleet had not been disrupted by bad weather, the United Irishmen might have had a chance. Instead, the authorities were given time to embark on a ruthless campaign of disarmament. The damage inflicted on the organization ensured that when rebellion broke out in May, 1798, it was fragmented and localized, being confined for the most part to east Ulster and, especially, County Wexford. Some French support was dispatched, but it came too late to alter the outcome, and the Crown forces won the day. The political initiative remained firmly in the hands of the establishment and the 1790s concluded, not with the declaration of the republic sought by the radicals, but with a legislative union.

## Radicalism and Rebellion in the 1790s

← French invasion forces, 1796–98

▨ Temporarily occupied by French forces, Aug.–Oct. 1798

— Humbert's invasion of Connacht

■ Main area of United Irish activity, 1797–98

▧ Main area of Defender activity

✕ Major 1798 battles

*Oct. 1798*
*Bompard and Wolfe Tone intercepted before they could land*

*Sept. 1798*
*General Ray and Napper Tandy land, then depart after a few days*

DONEGAL

DERRY

U l s t e r

ANTRIM
Antrim
*June 1798* ✕

TYRONE

*Lough Neagh*

Ballynahinch
✕ *June 1798*

D O W N

*Aug. 1798*
*Humbert*

Killala ●

SLIGO

Dromahair ●

FERMANAGH

ARMAGH

MONAGHAN

LEITRIM

CAVAN

LOUTH

Castlebar ●
Foxford
MAYO ✕ *August 1798*

ROSCOMMON

Ballinamuck
✕ *Sept. 1798*

LONGFORD

C o n n a c h t

Tara ✕ *May 1798*

MEATH

WESTMEATH

Athlone ●

L e i n s t e r

DUBLIN

GALWAY

Galway ●

KING'S CO.

KILDARE

Dublin ●

53°

CLARE

QUEEN'S CO.

The Curragh
✕ *May 1798*

WICKLOW

Tinahely ●
✕ *June 1798*
Arklow

Limerick ●

Carnew ●
✕ *May 1798*
Bunclody ● ● Gorey

CARLOW

✕ Vinegar Hill
*June 1798*

LIMERICK

TIPPERARY

KILKENNY

WEXFORD

New Ross
✕ *June 1798*

Wexford ●

Tralee ●

CORK

WATERFORD

Waterford ●

M u n s t e r

KERRY

Cork ●

Youghal ●

Bantry ●

*Dec. 1796*
*Hoche.*
*Disrupted by weather*

N

0        20 km
0        20 miles

# Catholic Emancipation and Repeal

FOLLOWING the repeal between 1778 and 1792 of the bulk of the laws restricting the liberty of Catholics to worship, to own and lease land, to educate their children and to enter the professions, and the enfranchisement in 1793 of Catholic forty-shilling freeholders, the major remaining infraction of Catholic civil rights was the prohibition on their sitting in parliament. Hopes were raised in 1794–95 and in 1799–1800 that Catholic emancipation would not be long delayed, but Protestant conservatives in both kingdoms remained firmly opposed. In 1801, William Pitt failed to overcome royal opposition and was unable to honor an assurance he had given Catholics during the union negotiations. Together Catholics and Whig sympathizers like Henry Grattan tried to overcome Protestant resistance by proposing a Crown 'veto' over ecclesiastical appointments, but this only helped to fragment the pro-emancipation lobby. For many Catholics, including the bishops, the proposed veto powers went too far, and Daniel O'Connell emerged as the leader of those Catholics who chose to endure exclusion rather than to accept conditional emancipation.

By the early 1820s, O'Connell had concluded that a new strategy was necessary and, following the foundation of the Catholic Association in 1823, he oversaw its transformation into one of the most remarkable agencies of popular politicization yet seen in Ireland or Europe. As a consequence, in the landmark general election of 1826, Catholics throughout the country cast off the bonds of deference and returned MPs sympathetic to their cause. Catholic confidence was further boosted two years later when O'Connell won a remarkable by-election victory in County Clare, and fearful that the resultant rise in sectarian animosity could precipitate serious civil discord, the duke of Wellington persuaded the reluctant George IV to concede to Catholics the right to sit in parliament.

Emboldened by this, in 1830 O'Connell launched a campaign to repeal the Act of Union. The campaign did not register the decisive impression he hoped for, but it provided him with an issue around which he could organize an Irish party at Westminster. On the back of some striking electoral successes in the early and mid-1830s, O'Connell forged a working alliance with the Whigs to secure a number of adminstrative and political reforms. However, following the return of the Tories to power in 1841, he devoted his energies to repeal. Supported by an energetic group of intellectual nationalists called the Young Irelanders, by the Church and by his own formidable Repeal Association, O'Connell organized a series of 'monster meetings' in 1843 with the object of compelling the government to concede Ireland 'full and prompt justice or repeal'. Ministers, however, were unyielding, and following the proscription of the meeting scheduled for Clontarf in October and O'Connell's subsequent imprisonment, he spent his final years vainly trying to retrieve lost ground.

*Below: Daniel O'Connell, known as 'The Liberator,' was one of the most charismatic leaders of his generation and enjoyed a reputation as a libertarian that extended far beyond Ireland's shores.*

## Catholic Emancipation and Repeal

*Catholic rent per county, 1824–25*

| | |
|---|---|
| ▨ | More than £700 |
| ▨ | £301 to £700 |
| ▨ | £101 to £300 |
| ☐ | £100 or less |

*Liberal electoral Clubs, 1826–30*

| | |
|---|---|
| ◉ | Town |
| ● | County |

| | |
|---|---|
| *Co. Dublin 1826* | Electoral victories for Catholic Association by constituency |
| *1832* | Electoral victories for Repeal Party, 1832, by constituency |
| (2) | 2 MPs elected |
| △ | Monster meetings, 1843 |

### Catholic rent, 1824–25
**Provincial totals**

| | |
|---|---|
| Leinster | £ 7,043 |
| Ulster | £ 1,837 |
| Munster | £ 6,571 |
| Connacht | £ 1,408 |

Map labels:

DONEGAL
DERRY
ANTRIM
Ulster
TYRONE
Lough Neagh
DOWN
FERMANAGH
*Co. Monaghan 1826* ARMAGH
*Co. Armagh 1826*
MONAGHAN
Newry
Sligo △
Carrickmacross
△ Dundalk
SLIGO
LEITRIM
CAVAN
✕ *Battle of Ballybay, Sept. 1828*
LOUTH
*Co. Louth 1826 1832 (2)*
Castlebar △ MAYO
ROSCOMMON
Longford △
△ Kells
*Co. Meath 1832 (2)*
△ Drogheda *1832*
△ Bellewstown
*Co. Mayo 1826*
*Co. Roscommon 1826 1832*
LONGFORD
*Co. Meath*
MEATH
Connacht
Clifden △
△ Tuam
WESTMEATH
Trim △
DUBLIN
L. Owel △ Mullingar
Tara
GALWAY
Athlone ◉ △
*Co. Westmeath 1826 1832*
*Co. Kildare 1832*
Clontarf △
*Co. Dublin 1826 1832*
◉ Dublin *1832 (2)*
Galway ● △
*1832 (2)*
Tullamore △
KING'S CO.
*King's Co. 1832*
Naas ◉
KILDARE
△ The Curragh
WICKLOW
Queen's Co. *1832*
△ Donnybrook
△ Baltinglass
△ Mullaghmast
*Co. Clare 1828*
QUEEN'S CO.
Portlaoise ●
Carlow *1832*
CLARE ● Ennis △
*1832 (2)*
△ Nenagh
TIPPERARY
*Co. Kilkenny 1832*
CARLOW
*Co. Carlow 1832*
Limerick ●
*1832 (2)* △ Murroe
*Co. Tipperary 1832 (2)*
Kilkenny *1832* △
WEXFORD
Rathkeale △ LIMERICK
KILKENNY
△ Enniscorthy
*Co. Limerick 1826*
△ Cashel *1832*
Clonmel *1832*
New Ross *1832*
● Tralee *1832*
△ Charleville
*Co. Waterford 1826*
Wexford *1832* ●
KERRY
*Co. Cork 1832 (2)*
△ Mallow
Lismore △ *1832*
Waterford ◉ △
*Co. Kerry 1832 (2)*
Munster
WATERFORD
Youghal △ *1832*
CORK ●
△ ◉ Cork *1832 (2)*

N

| 0 | 20 km |
| 0 | 20 miles |

# Nineteenth-Century Catholicism

DESPITE THE Penal Laws, it is clear from the returns made by Catholic bishops to Dublin Castle that the Church in 1800 was better provided with priests than it had been a century earlier. It was also embarked on a campaign of church refurbishment and construction that was to see the humble thatched dwellings identified with the Penal era being replaced by the ornate, prominent stone edifices of the 19th century. The pace of this development varied from diocese to diocese, and within each diocese from parish to parish, depending on its leadership and resources. Widespread improvements commenced in the second half of the 18th century and accelerated in the early 19th, with the wealthier dioceses of Dublin and Cashel progressing more rapidly than those of Tuam and Armagh.

One important index of the growing strength of the Catholic Church is provided by the swelling ranks of its priests and nuns. In the first half of the 19th century their numbers were insufficient to permit the Church to administer equally to all its members: in 1840 there was one priest per 3,000 people. This problem was most acute in Connacht, and it is not surprising that in 1834 the Commissioners of Public Instruction found the church attendance here lower than elsewhere. In Connacht also there was the strongest adherence to popular religious practices associated with wakes, patterns and holy wells. These practices were a primary target for the burgeoning ranks of the Maynooth-trained secular clergy who oversaw the gradual countrywide extension of the Tridentine orthodoxies laid down by Reformist bishops like Murray of Dublin and Doyle of Kildare and Leighlin. Also, the Great Famine dealt its heaviest blows in the sectors of Irish society in which such practices were most deeply entrenched, and reduced the priest-people ratio in 1870 to 1:1,250. This alleviated endemic problems of clerical indiscipline and paved the way for the provision to all Catholics of a comprehensive religious service from birth to death. Indeed, priests became their communities' moral policemen, and as the Church continued to grow in wealth, numbers and influence, it assumed responsibility for an increasing network of social functions—schools, orphanages, hospitals, asylums and so on—through which it conveyed its message.

19th-Century Catholicism

— Ecclesiastical provinces
- - - Diocesan boundary

*Number of people per priest,
1845, per diocese (after Kerr)*

3001 or more
2501 to 3000
2001 to 2500
1501 to 2000
1500 or less

Diocesan cathedrals
with dates of
construction

*Number of clergy in each
diocese*

100
50 — 1800
0 — 1845

Letterkenny
RAPHOE
Derry 1851–73
DERRY
DOWN & CONNOR
Belfast 1860–66

A r m a g h

CLOGHER
ARMAGH
Armagh 1840–73
DROMORE
Monaghan 1861–92
Newry 1825–29

KILMORE

Sligo 1869–74
Ballina 1827–92
KILLALA
Ballaghaderreen
ACHONRY 1855–60
ELPHIN
ARDAGH & CLONMACNOISE
Cavan 1862
MEATH

T u a m

Tuam 1827–37
GALWAY
Galway 1816
KILMACDUAGH
CLONFERT
Loughrea 1897–1902
A & C
Longford 1840–56
Mullingar 1831–36
Dublin 1815–25
KILDARE & LEIGHLIN

*Galway united
with Kilmacduagh
and Kilfenora in 1883*

KILFENORA

KILLALOE

D u b l i n

DUBLIN

Ennis 1828–43
Limerick 1856–61
LIMERICK
Thurles 1809
CASHEL & EMLY
OSSORY
Carlow 1828–33
Kilkenny 1843–57
FERNS
Enniscorthy 1809

C a s h e l

KERRY
CLOYNE
Killarney 1842–55
WATERFORD & LISMORE
Waterford 1793–96

Cork 1799–1808
Cobh 1868–79
CORK
ROSS *Linked with
Cloyne to 1850*
Skibbereen 1824–27

*Lough
Neagh*

N

0    20 km
0    20 miles

# The Pre-Famine Economy

THE STRONG growth registered by the Irish economy in the second half of the 18th century and in the early years of the 19th came to an abrupt halt in the mid-1810s. The deflationary fiscal policy of the post-Napoleonic War government hit the banking sector especially hard, but the decline in the volume of linen and in the value of agricultural goods exported in the late 1810s indicates that the problem went deeper. The crisis was most acute in the countryside, which was affected not only by the agricultural slump, but by the general economic downturn, for much of Ireland's manufacturing was domestically based. It was compounded too by the country's demographic position: by 1820 its rising population neared 7 million.

Above: *Weighing potatoes, the staple of the agrarian community. Reliance on this single crop, together with the relative unsophistication of the Irish economy, left country people, particularly in the west, vulnerable to sudden change.*

In the late 18th century this had been accommodated by expanding employment in linen and tillage, and by the subdivision of holdings by landowners and middle-men. So long as domestic and international conditions were favourable, and the landless and landed labourers (cottiers) who constituted 56 per cent of the labour in 1841 could rely on the potato, this rising population was not a cause of concern. However, as rent arrears climbed sharply in the early 19th century, it quickly became apparent that substantial holdings were more economically viable than small tenancies. Evictions increased, but the sheer number of tenants on most estates and their mutual solidarity prevented all but the most determined land-lords from restructuring land occupancy along sound economic lines. Cottiers and labourers eked out a precarious existence, but while the potato remained free from disease they remained reasonably well nourished.

In 1841 farmers with more than fifty acres represented only 4 per cent of the labour force. They had a ready market in industrial Britain for their grain, cat-tle and butter. Ulster linen-workers also found a market in Britain, but were threatened by mechanization. From the 1820s the development of machine-spin-ning and particularly of wet spinning forced a dramatic contraction in hand spinning in north Leinster, north Connacht and south, west and central Ulster. It appeared briefly that linen might be displaced by cotton, but the construction of a linen mill in 1828 on the site of a burnt-out Belfast cotton works indicated that the industry had a brighter future, and the building of another sixty in the northeast within a decade confirmed this.

This was the only area of Ireland to industrialize. Elsewhere, there were suc-cessful individual enterprises such as the Guinness brewery, but few successful industrial sectors. The proportion of the population engaged in trade and manufacture between 1821 and 1841 fell by 15 per cent, demonstrating the general weakness of the economy.

## Pre-Famine Economy

*Regional occupation —
main employments, 1841*

- Linen weavers
- Linen spinners
- Agricultural labourers and other agricultural activities
- Tradesmen and domestic servants

*Percentage of growth in
population by county, 1821–41*

- more than 26
- 23 to 26
- 15 to 22
- less than 15

*Main towns and cities:
population*

20,000
10,000
0
1821
1841

DONEGAL 19%

Derry

DERRY 15%

TYRONE 20%

ANTRIM 33%

Belfast

Ulster

FERMANAGH 19%

Armagh 18%

ARMAGH 15%

DOWN 11%

Newry

MONAGHAN 15%

SLIGO

Sligo

LEITRIM 24%

CAVAN 25%

LOUTH 8%

Dundalk

MAYO 33%

ROSCOMMON 21%

LONGFORD 7%

MEATH 15%

Drogheda

Connacht

GALWAY

Galway 31%

WESTMEATH 10%

Leinster

KING'S CO. 12%

KILDARE 16%

DUBLIN

Dublin 11%

CLARE 38%

QUEEN'S CO. 15%

WICKLOW 14%

Limerick

LIMERICK 20%

TIPPERARY 26%

Carlow

CARLOW 9%

Kilkenny

KILKENNY 11%

WEXFORD 18%

Clonmel

Waterford

Wexford

Tralee

KERRY 36%

CORK 17%

WATERFORD 25%

Munster

Cork

### Population growth, 1821–41, by province

| | |
|---|---|
| Leinster | 12.3% |
| Ulster | 19.4% |
| Munster | 23.8% |
| Connacht | 27.8% |

N

0 ___ 20 km

0 ___ 20 miles

# Emigration to 1845

THOUGH THE Irish are today widely perceived as an emigrant people, emigration from the island is in fact only a comparatively recent phenomenon. Prior to the 18th century, the country gained more people than it lost.

The best known of 18th-century Irish emigration was that of the Ulster Scots, who were tempted by the opportunities in the American colonies, and chose to settle there in small numbers from the late 1710s, rising to as many as 50,000 in the early 1770s. Much of this emigration, distinct from the seasonal migrations to Britain and Newfoundland, was by relatively affluent families, but the practice of indentured servitude provided a means by which the poor and restless could also leave.

The American War of Independence (1775–83) temporarily prevented access to what had become the main destination for Irish emigrants. By the early 1770s emigration to America was an established aspect of Irish life, though it was small enough to make little impression on the fast-growing population.

From 1827, the number of emigrants to North America exceeded 20,000 for the first time since the 1780s, and the trend was upwards. In 1831–32, it reached 65,000 for the first time, and average annual emigration to North America exceeded 65,000 between 1841 and 1845. In total, almost one million people left Ireland for North America between 1815 and 1845, and while a majority of these first set foot on Canadian soil, this was a reflection of the cost of their passage, not their choice of destination.

While to reach the United States was the ambition of most Irish emigrants, an increasing number were also drawn to industrial Britain. There were significant concentrations of Irish in several English cities by 1800, but these were dwarfed by the 500,000 or so emigrants that moved to Britain in the early 19th century. This trend may reflect the strong tradition of seasonal migration to Britain that had been established in the 18th century.

Below: *People gather at the Government Inspector's Office determined to take a ship for America. Engraving from the* Illustrated London News, *July, 1850.*

Irish convicts were transported to Australia from the late 1780s, when America's newly-won independence ruled it out as an option. Between the 1780s and 1845, Australia was the destination of between 50,000 and 65,000 Irish felons. A minority, among them some United Irishmen, were political prisoners, but most were common criminals exiled by a penal system that preferred expulsion to the cost of imprisonment.

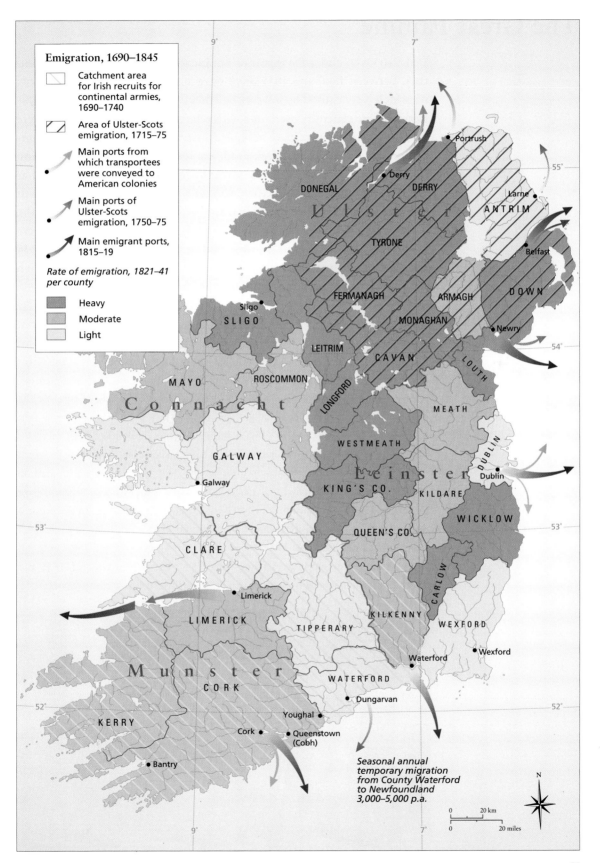

**Emigration, 1690–1845**

Catchment area for Irish recruits for continental armies, 1690–1740

Area of Ulster-Scots emigration, 1715–75

Main ports from which transportees were conveyed to American colonies

Main ports of Ulster-Scots emigration, 1750–75

Main emigrant ports, 1815–19

*Rate of emigration, 1821–41 per county*

Heavy

Moderate

Light

DONEGAL
Derry
DERRY
Portrush
Larne
ANTRIM
Belfast
Ulster
TYRONE
FERMANAGH
ARMAGH
DOWN
SLIGO
Sligo
MONAGHAN
Newry
LEITRIM
CAVAN
LOUTH
MAYO
ROSCOMMON
LONGFORD
Connacht
MEATH
WESTMEATH
GALWAY
Leinster
DUBLIN
Galway
KING'S CO.
KILDARE
Dublin
WICKLOW
QUEEN'S CO.
CLARE
CARLOW
Limerick
KILKENNY
WEXFORD
LIMERICK
TIPPERARY
Munster
Waterford
Wexford
CORK
WATERFORD
Dungarvan
KERRY
Youghal
Cork
Queenstown (Cobh)
Bantry

*Seasonal annual temporary migration from County Waterford to Newfoundland 3,000–5,000 p.a.*

N

0   20 km
0   20 miles

# The Great Famine

IRELAND LIVED under the threat of famine throughout the early 19th century. Between 1800 and 1845 there were some sixteen food crises, most of which were caused by adverse weather conditions. Because the emergencies were generally overcome with relatively modest loss of life, there was no reason to anticipate an epic disaster, and the fact that the country annually produced enough food, not just to feed its own population but to export a healthy surplus, gives the lie to those who maintain that the Great Famine was a disaster waiting to happen. Population growth had already declined appreciably from its 18th-century peak, and by the early 1840s increasing numbers were emigrating. The rural poor were nevertheless vulnerable to disaster, and in 1845 it came from Europe in the form of an incurable fungal disease, 'Phytophthera infestans,' which decimated their staple food stuff, the potato crop.

The blight spread rapidly because of the wet harvest season, and 40 per cent of the crop was destroyed. This was enough to plunge the country into crisis, though imports of Indian meal at first kept mortality within bounds. If the blight had not recurred, the setback of 1845 would not have been much more consequential than any of the previous regional crises. Unfortunately, in three of the following four years the potato blight again took a heavy toll, with the result that when relief from private and official sources proved inadequate, tens of thousands died annually from malnutrition and epidemic disease. According to recent calculations approximately one million people died, of which an estimated 40 per cent came from Connacht, 30 per cent from Munster, 21 per cent from Ulster and 9 per cent from Leinster. Inevitably the crisis was most severe in the poorest areas: death and emigration reduced the population to 6.5 million, with the proportion of landholdings of less than five acres falling from 35 to 20 per cent, and those of fifteen or more acres rising from 31 to 48 per cent between 1841 and 1851. Post-Famine rural Ireland was to be quite different as a consequence.

*Right: The poor and destitute gather outside the gates of a workhouse hoping for shelter and food. By 1847 the local systems of relief were utterly overwhelmed by the magnitude of the crisis.*

Distressed Poor Law
Unions, 1848–51

Unions in receipt of
largest soup rations,
1847 (after Kinealy)

Ulster

Connacht

Leinster

Munster

DONEGAL

DERRY

ANTRIM

Ulster

TYRONE

DOWN

FERMANAGH

MONAGHAN

ARMAGH

SLIGO

LEITRIM

CAVAN

LOUTH

MAYO

Connacht

ROSCOMMON

LONGFORD

MEATH

WESTMEATH

KILDARE    Dublin

DUBLIN

GALWAY

KING'S CO.

Leinster

QUEEN'S CO.

WICKLOW

CLARE

KILKENNY

CARLOW

WEXFORD

LIMERICK

TIPPERARY

Munster

WATERFORD

KERRY

CORK

**Numbers in Mullingar workhouse
1845–1850**

2,500
2,000
1,500
1,000
5000

1845  1847  1848  1849  1850

**The Great Famine**

*Excess Death Rate, 1846–51
in percentages (after Mokyr)*

20 to 33

10 to 19

5 to 9

1 to 4

Population gain

*County population, 1841–51
(census figures)*

100,000            1841

50,000             1851

0

# The Decline of the Irish Language

**The Irish language, of which Scottish Gaelic and Manx are dialects, is of Celtic and ultimately Indo-European origin, and has been spoken in Ireland for perhaps 2,500 years. Although it began to exhibit some minor Norse influences in the aftermath of the Viking invasions, its position as the language of Ireland only underwent serious challenge with the introduction of substantial communities of English speakers in the aftermath of the English invasion in the late 12th century.**

Nevertheless, Irish retained its dominance, and, indeed, by the 14th century was spoken by an increasing number of settlers, with Gaelic culture undergoing a considerable resurgence in spite of attempts by the Dublin government to legislate against it. English language and influence were never eradicated, however, especially from the towns, and the Tudor reconquest put Irish very much on the defensive. By the early 17th century, the native aristocracy, the principal patrons of Gaelic culture, had been overthrown, and the language lost its ascendancy. Plantations of new English-speaking settlers and a comprehensive redistribution of landownership following the Cromwellian and Williamite wars meant that the new proprietorial, professional and mercantile classes were English-speaking virtually without exception.

Although Gaelic literature survived, and its merits increasingly gained an antiquarian appreciation, it was now predominantly the expression of an underclass, and for those anxious to gain social or economic advancement a knowledge of English was essential. Ironically, as the population began to rise rapidly, by the early 19th century there were probably more Irish-speakers than at any time previously (four million or more), but they were the poorest sections of society, and an accelerating abandonment of Irish had begun well before the Great Famine struck in the mid-1840s. Death and massive emigration had the

*Below: Early premises of Conradh na Gaeilge (the Gaelic League) in Sackville Street, around the turn of the century.*

effect of decimating the language, aided by a hostile education system and a largely unsympathetic Church, so that by the end of the century its future seemed bleak.

At this point, however, a vibrant language revival movement emerged in the form of the Gaelic League (*Conradh na Gaeilge*), interest growing in tandem with the demand for political independence. The establishment of the Irish Free State in 1922 had the not entirely healthy effect of institutionalizing the language movement (except in the six counties which became Northern Ireland) and government efforts to promote Irish, especially by maintaining the viability of the Gaeltacht, the remaining Irish-speaking areas, and insisting on compulsory instruction in schools, have thus far attained only limited success. Perhaps the best hope for the language's future lies in the enthusiasm which individual groups of parents are showing for the provision of all-Irish primary education for their children in the form of *Gaelscoileanna*.

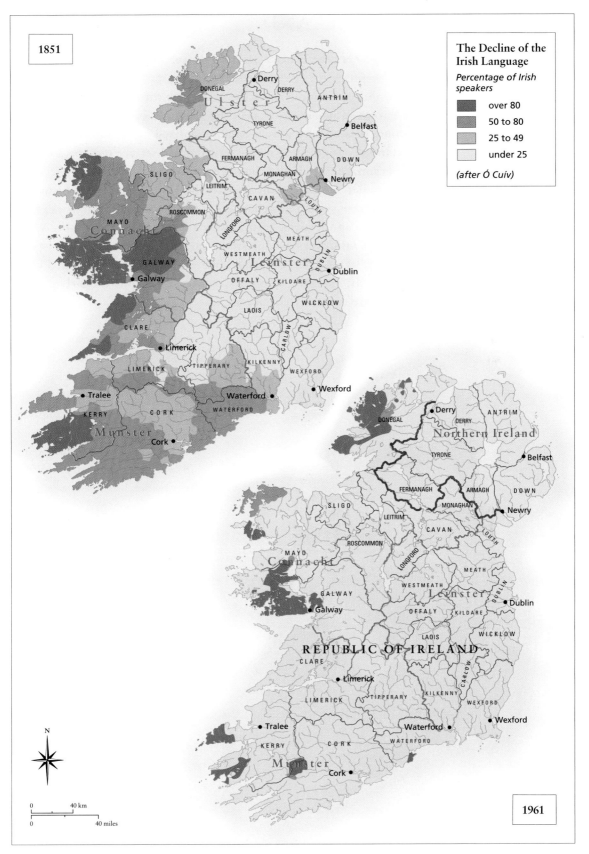

1851

**The Decline of the Irish Language**

*Percentage of Irish speakers*

- over 80
- 50 to 80
- 25 to 49
- under 25

*(after Ó Cuív)*

1961

N

| 0 | 40 km |
| 0 | 40 miles |

# PART V: MODERN IRELAND

*Gabriel Doherty*

AT FIRST SIGHT the history of Ireland over the course of the last 150 years manifests many similarities with the process of political, economic and social modernization evident in the evolution of its western European neighbors during the same period. A market-oriented economy characterized by a commercialized agricultural sector and substantially augmented manufacturing and service sectors; a literate population, increasingly urbanized, who live longer, marry less and have smaller families compared to their forebears; a sophisticated social welfare system designed to cater for the multifarious needs of its citizens; and a social culture which has become daily more variegated and influenced by international trends—in all these respects and more Ireland has changed since the Famine and changed quite dramatically, but only, it appears, to become less distinctively national and more routinely cosmopolitan.

*Below: Charles Stewart Parnell entered parliament in 1875 and was active in the 'obstructionist' faction of the Home Rule Party; their intention was to obstruct the day-to-day business of parliament in order to highlight Irish issues.*

Other important changes should also be noted, most notably the dramatic decline in the island's population since the Famine (which stands in stark contrast to the unprecedented rate of expansion in the pre-Famine era, and also to the expansion evident elsewhere in Europe since the middle of the last century) and the formal partition of the island in 1920 into two distinct political entities. This latter development in particular, although in some respects only the formal political confirmation of a pattern of regional social and economic differentiation evident for over a century, nonetheless marked a significant point of departure for the subsequent history of the island, albeit not a very propitious one.

Such changes notwithstanding, however, there are characteristics of Irish life which have withstood the passage of time and which continue to set off Irish politics and society from those obtaining in other countries. The issues of ownership, dis-

Below: *Presidents John F. Kennedy and Éamon de Valera together during JFK's triumphant visit to Ireland in June 1963. He was seen as the supreme symbol of Irish-American success and was received like a conquering hero.*

Below: *Dr. Noel Browne, seen here being chased by police following a protest outside the American embassy in Dublin in the 1960s, had been Minister for Health from 1948 to 1951. A passionate socialist and radical, he had spearheaded the campaign which effectively eradicated tuberculosis as an epidemic disease in Ireland. In doing so, he removed one of the country's greatest scourges.*

tribution and utilization of land have proved to be as contentious in this era as they were in the more distant past. The 'quiet revolution,' by which ownership of land was transferred in the late 19th and early 20th centuries from landlord to tenant, was effected with less difficulty than many expected bearing in mind its uniquely controversial history, but changes in formal patterns of tenure were less significant than the contemporaneous and accelerated shift from arable to pastoral usage. While similar developments were taking place elsewhere, the social consequences of such a reorientation were perhaps more problematic for Ireland than for any other western European country, given the complex political context within which it took place, although one should note that the political disturbances of the period between 1915 and 1923 were not, in the main, economically determined.

Concern with land, however, has not been the only issue which has served to highlight the continuities between the pre- and post-Famine eras. The enduring cultural achievements of the Irish people, exemplified in the international acclaim accorded to such outstanding literary figures as Oscar Wilde, George Bernard Shaw, W.B. Yeats, James Joyce, Samuel Beckett and, more recently, Seamus Heaney and Frank McCourt, have also been widely attested to. Less straightforward has been the intellectual legacy of modern Irish nationalism which has provided the inspiration for some of the most dramatic developments of the period, most obviously the achievement of political independence for the greater part of the island under the terms of the 1921 Anglo-Irish Treaty, but which, in common with the equally problematic phenomenon of unionism, has left a complex and frequently divisive mark on the political and social landscape of the northeastern part of the island in particular.

The form of Ireland's relationship with Britain has thus been one of the constant, defining features of the modern Irish experience, north and south, but the fluctuating fortunes of that relationship should not obscure the more nuanced but equally interesting links which have been forged between

Ireland and the wider world over the course of the last century and a half. The most tangible of those bonds have come in the shape of its people, the hundreds of thousands of emigrants who, for a variety of reasons, left their homeland to seek a new life elsewhere. Many of these, particularly during the middle of the 20th century, settled in the neighboring isle but for the earlier period and again more recently other, more distant destinations have figured prominently—most obviously in America but also in Canada, Australia, New Zealand and elsewhere. Not that their departure meant that

Below: *Charles Haughey, the most charismatic and controversial Irish Taoiseach of modern times.*

they or their offspring lost interest in matters affecting the 'mother country'; on the contrary, these communities sustained a vibrant sense of Irish nationality in their adopted homes, albeit one attenuated by the conditions of the host society.

In addition to the legacy of the Irish abroad, numerous bonds have also served to incorporate the Irish experience into that of mainland Europe during these eventful years, a mutual interaction given institutional recognition in 1973 with the entry of both the Republic of Ireland and Northern Ireland (as part of the United Kingdom) into the European Economic Community (subsequently the European Union). It is the economic impact of this association which has, perhaps not surprisingly, received the lion's share of attention over the last quarter of a century but this should not blind one to its powerful social and political undercurrents—undercurrents which may, in the fullness of time, come to be regarded as its most enduring legacy.

It is, however, the story of what happened, and those who remained, in Ireland with which we are most concerned here. In this respect the transfer of political power from London to administrations in both Dublin and (to a lesser extent) Belfast in the early 1920s provided an opportunity for these governments to formulate policies designed to promote the specific interests of the Irish people. The development of two distinctive socio-political regimes north and south of the border—the former self-consciously British and Protestant, the latter explicitly Gaelic and Catholic in its cultural formation—bore testimony to the deep divisions within the country which predated even the Famine, but even here the enduring ties of history between the two political areas should not be ignored. It is one of the enduring ironies of modern Irish history that the regional differences within the island—east/west as well as north/south—are in many respects less manifest now than in the middle of the 19th century, but are widely known and more

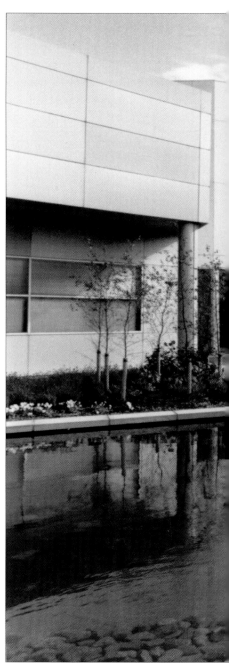

Above and right: *During the late 1980s and 1990s Ireland has enjoyed outstanding economic success, growing consistently around 6-7 per cent. The high standard of education has attracted inward investment from the global economy, backed by infrastructural investment from the EU. The establishment of new activities, such as computers and financial services, has led to an increasing sophistication and diversification of opportunity, alongside Ireland's traditional and well-established industries.*

keenly felt, and it is in this context that the debate on national identify, the nature of the Irish quintessence, which has proliferated over the last century, must be studied.

In short, while the island of Ireland has undoubtedly experienced massive and at times painful social and political change since 1851, evidence of the pervasive influence of its historical inheritance is as much in evidence on its contemporary intellectual landscape as it is on its physical one.

# Post-Famine Emigration

THE FAMINE was a milestone in modern Irish history, not merely because of the sheer horror of the human suffering it carried in its wake (awful though this was) but also because it gave an added impetus to the development of profound social changes which had become evident during the years immediately prior to 1845.

Of these changes it was perhaps the scale of emigration which was the most important. So huge was this emigration that Ireland, which had experienced substantial population expansion over the course of the previous 100 years, now entered a period of population decline which had no contemporary comparison in Europe and which was to continue almost unchecked for well over a century. This phenomenon affected all creeds and classes and touched all parts of the country, although the poorer elements of the Catholic agricultural population of the south and west manifested the greatest relative decline, with Munster experiencing the largest absolute losses. The scale of female emigration was particularly noticeable, with the number of female emigrants at times outnumbering their male counterparts (contrary to the experience of most other countries).

While some emigrants settled in the growing industrial towns across the Irish Sea, most found themselves embarked on the hazardous sea journey towards a new life in North America, and in particular the United States. Initially finding themselves the subject of suspicion and distrust in their adopted homeland they nonetheless quickly adjusted and made an enormous contribution to the subsequent development of the country. Notwithstanding the fact that they had in the main come from an agricultural background, most of these emigrants settled in large cities on the east coast of America, and while the numbers returning to Ireland remained small in comparison to other nationalities, yet they retained an interest in Irish affairs which has persisted to the present day.

Back in Ireland other important demographic trends were becoming noticeable. In particular the marriage rate, which had been quite high prior to the

Below: 'Steerage emigrants,' a wood engraving by Arthur Boyd Houghton, published in the Graphic, March, 1869, shows poor emigrants sailing the cheap steerage passage to North America.

Famine, now slowly declined (although as can be seen from the map this process did not proceed at the same pace throughout the island). This was due to the increase in the number of individuals who never married, together with an increase in the average age at the time. Notwithstanding this significant development the birth rate remained well above the European average, although this was also subject to significant geographic variation.

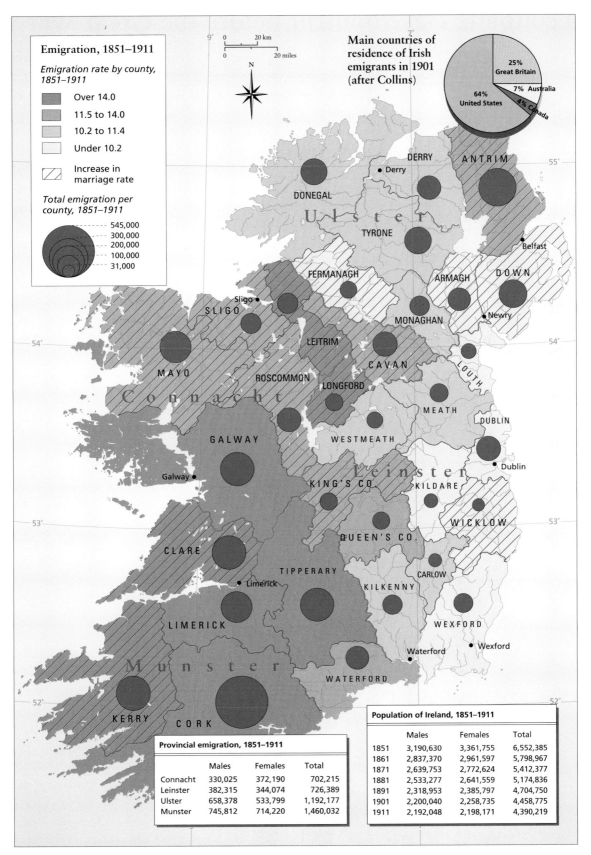

## Emigration, 1851–1911

*Emigration rate by county, 1851–1911*

- Over 14.0
- 11.5 to 14.0
- 10.2 to 11.4
- Under 10.2

Increase in marriage rate

*Total emigration per county, 1851–1911*

- 545,000
- 300,000
- 200,000
- 100,000
- 31,000

**Main countries of residence of Irish emigrants in 1901 (after Collins)**

- 25% Great Britain
- 7% Australia
- 4% Canada
- 64% United States

### Provincial emigration, 1851–1911

|          | Males   | Females | Total     |
|----------|---------|---------|-----------|
| Connacht | 330,025 | 372,190 | 702,215   |
| Leinster | 382,315 | 344,074 | 726,389   |
| Ulster   | 658,378 | 533,799 | 1,192,177 |
| Munster  | 745,812 | 714,220 | 1,460,032 |

### Population of Ireland, 1851–1911

|      | Males     | Females   | Total     |
|------|-----------|-----------|-----------|
| 1851 | 3,190,630 | 3,361,755 | 6,552,385 |
| 1861 | 2,837,370 | 2,961,597 | 5,798,967 |
| 1871 | 2,639,753 | 2,772,624 | 5,412,377 |
| 1881 | 2,533,277 | 2,641,559 | 5,174,836 |
| 1891 | 2,318,953 | 2,385,797 | 4,704,750 |
| 1901 | 2,200,040 | 2,258,735 | 4,458,775 |
| 1911 | 2,192,048 | 2,198,171 | 4,390,219 |

# Economic Development before the Great War

THE HUMAN changes which followed the Famine were accompanied (and indeed partly explained) by dramatic changes in the national economy. One of the most important of these was the acceleration of the shift in agricultural production away from small-scale intensive tillage operations towards a more extensive dairy system. There were many reasons for this development, which involved the frequently controversial consolidation of large numbers of small holdings into more substantial and efficient units. Undoubtedly the Irish climate played a part, being conducive to grazing, but the government also exercised a direct influence, particularly by means of the legislation which it passed in the aftermath of the Famine which simplified the rather cumbersome existing procedures for the transfer of the ownership of land.

Such chances, together with the now near-universal tendency for land to be inherited *en bloc* rather than be divided up among competing offspring, produced large numbers of individuals and families who could find no role in the new economic dispensation and who formed the bulk of the emigrants discussed earlier. In the north, however, the second major development in the Irish economy during the second part of the century—the growth of manufacturing industry in the area (particularly in Belfast and Derry)—provided for many an alternative to the emigrant ship. Large numbers of agricultural workers, both Catholic and Protestant, now settled in these cities, hoping to find work in the new ship-building yards or linen mills which were opening at that time. These workers frequently had to endure appalling working and living conditions, to which were added the tensions which had long characterized relations between the two major religious blocs in the area.

A number of other developments in the national economy must also be mentioned. In particular the Irish economy was becoming ever more integrated into the British economic sphere of influence, a development aided by the improved road, rail and port facilities which developed in the sixty years after the Famine. Irish economic activity generally became more commercially-oriented and moved decisively away from the subsistence-type of production which had characterized certain areas in the earlier decades of the century. Partly as a consequence of this development, living standards across the island gradually improved, although it did leave the economy rather vulnerable to changes in European and world markets over which it had little control.

Below: *Shipyard workers leaving the Harland and Wolff yard in Belfast at the end of a working day. Belfast and its environs were the center of Ireland's industrial revolution, thus marking the north off even more from the agricultural south and west.*

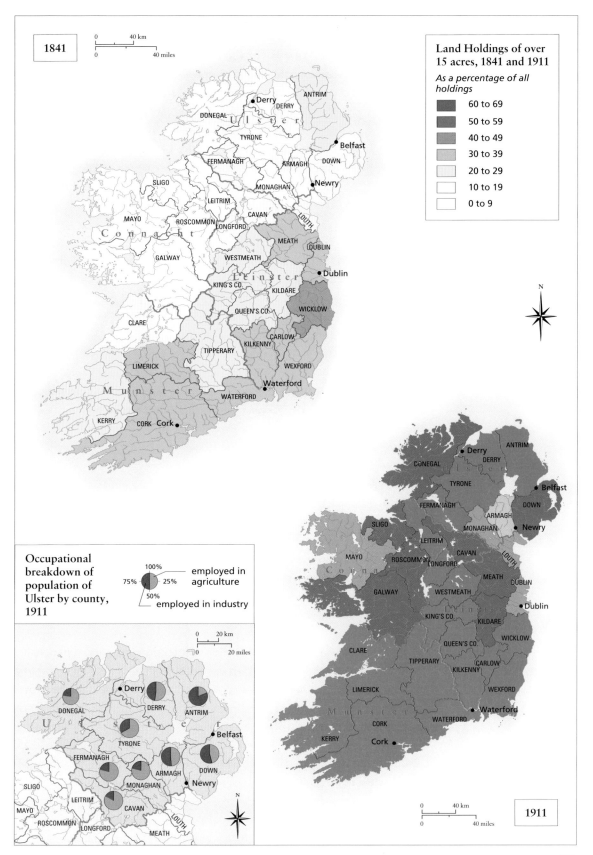

1841

0   40 km
0   40 miles

**Land Holdings of over 15 acres, 1841 and 1911**

*As a percentage of all holdings*

- 60 to 69
- 50 to 59
- 40 to 49
- 30 to 39
- 20 to 29
- 10 to 19
- 0 to 9

Occupational breakdown of population of Ulster by county, 1911

100%
75%   25%
50%
employed in agriculture
employed in industry

0   20 km
0   20 miles

1911

0   40 km
0   40 miles

# The Growth of Irish Nationalism

*Above:* Thomas Davis, editor of The Nation, *was a popular idealist and the chief ideologue of the Young Ireland movement.*

THE TRAUMA of the Famine and the consequent readjustments provided an important impetus to the growth of political and cultural nationalism in the country. Building on the foundations laid by the United Irishmen and Daniel O'Connell, a series of individuals and groups during the latter part of the 19th century sought to cultivate a nationalist consciousness which would be the precursor to new and distinctively Irish political and social arrangements.

The first of these bodies—the Young Ireland movement of the 1840s—provided a coherent if not necessarily programmatic doctrine of nationality which was to inspire later generations. After failed rebellions in 1848 and 1867, it was only in the 1870s and 1880s that demands for the recognition of Ireland's distinctive inheritance found practical political expression through the activities at Westminster of the Irish Parliamentary Party, under the leadership initially of Isaac Butt and subsequently (and most impressively) of Charles Stewart Parnell. That both these men were Protestants bestowed upon the movement a deceptively ecumenical façade—in practice Irish nationalism became increasingly defined with the majority Catholic community (a development mirrored by the growth in support amongst Protestants for the maintenance of the Union of 1800).

A number of gains were made by the Irish Party, particularly in the area of land reform which the government undertook in the hope that it would forestall the growth of separatist sentiment, but on the key issue of political reform no progress was made and the controversial downfall of Parnell following his involvement in a divorce case seemed to stymie such hopes for the foreseeable future. Some felt that such a development was the inevitable consequence of constitutional action, and a revolutionary wing to the nationalist movement, the Irish Republican Brotherhood (the 'Fenians') was developed, albeit with little overt popular support.

It was, however, not just in political terms that the new sense of nationality manifested itself. Developments such as the foundation of the Gaelic Athletic Association (1884), a body dedicated to the maintenance of traditional Irish sports, and of the Gaelic League (1893), which sought to stem the apparently inexorable decline of the Irish language, bore testimony to a dynamic perception of nationality independent of political arrangements, a perception which found enduring cultural expression in the varied works of the Irish 'literary renaissance' evident during these years. The foundation in 1905 of Sinn Féin, a broadly-based nationalist organisation with a distinctive economic agenda, was but the latest in a long line of such bodies, although it was arguably to become the most influential in the renewed drive towards political independence.

The Growth of Irish Nationalism

Winners of parliamentary seats, 1895

- Anti-Parnellite Nationalist
- Parnellite Nationalist
- Liberal Unionist
- Unionist
- Liberal

Number of Gaelic Athletic Association clubs per county, 1907–08 and 1937:

40
20
0

1907–08
1937

# Government Policy

*Above: This well-known staged photograph features a means rarely used in case of eviction for non-payment of rent: the battering ram.*

THE GROWTH of nationalist sentiment presented the British government with severe difficulties. On the one hand the refusal to make concessions to the burgeoning nationalist lobby ran the risk of alienating the moderate majority; on the other, to give in to such demands raised the possibility of further, perhaps unpalatable demands.

The government's response had two elements. On the one hand it enacted wide-ranging social reforms where these were deemed to be compatible with existing constitutional arrangements. These reforms included the Land Acts (which essentially transferred ownership from landlord to tenant), the disestablishment of the Church of Ireland (1869), the establishment of a number of state agencies to assist with the task of developing the poorest areas of the country, and so on. In its latter stages this policy was accurately described as 'killing Home Rule by kindness,' that is, the removal of the social grievances which were felt to underpin the demand for political separation.

However the government proved itself willing to employ coercive methods whenever the political situation became unacceptably tense. This strategy was particularly evident during the so-called 'Land War' of 1879-82, when a number of individuals and organizations, notably the 'Land League' led by Michael Davitt, were the object of official harassment, and also during the 'Plan of Campaign' from 1886-92, which also focused on the key issue of land reform.

Two attempts were made to find a solution to the political question. In 1885 Gladstone, the Liberal Prime Minister, introduced a Home Rule Bill, which sought to bestow very limited powers on an all-Ireland Parliament. Even this was too much for Conservatives and Unionists, who launched a vigorous campaign of opposition to the Bill, which was defeated when the Liberal Party split on the issue in 1886. A second attempt by Gladstone to pass the Bill failed in 1893 when the measure was vetoed by the Conservative-dominated House of Lords.

For the next twenty years the Home Rule issue dropped off a political agenda dominated by the ruling Conservative Party, and attention in Ireland switched to social and economic issues. However the political and emotional capital invested in Home Rule by both Irish nationalists and British Liberals meant that the return of that latter party to power would inevitably witness a resurgence of interest in the question.

| Land Legislation, 1870–1903 | |
|---|---|
| 1870 | Made customary tenant right enforceable at law and provided compensation for disturbance. |
| 1881 | Concession of the 'Three Fs': right of free sale; judicial power to fix rents; conversion of ordinary tenancies to fixed tenancies. |
| 1885 | Allowed land commission to lend to tenants to purchase holdings from landlords. |
| 1903 | Wyndham's Act. Provided for long-term low-interest government loans to buy out landlords' interests. This crucial piece of legislation effectively ended the land question and created the typical 20th-century pattern of independent family farms. |

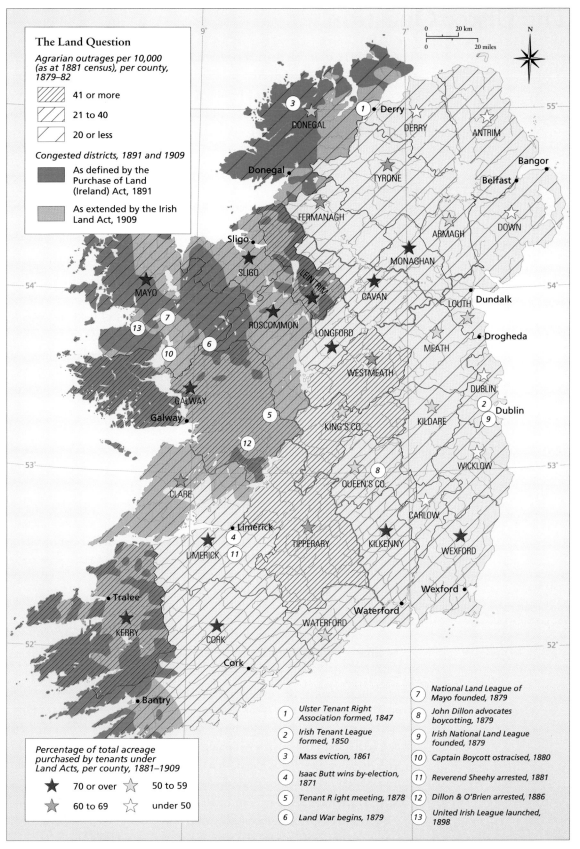

The Land Question

Agrarian outrages per 10,000 (as at 1881 census), per county, 1879–82

- 41 or more
- 21 to 40
- 20 or less

Congested districts, 1891 and 1909

- As defined by the Purchase of Land (Ireland) Act, 1891
- As extended by the Irish Land Act, 1909

Percentage of total acreage purchased by tenants under Land Acts, per county, 1881–1909

- ★ 70 or over
- ★ 60 to 69
- ☆ 50 to 59
- ☆ under 50

1. Ulster Tenant Right Association formed, 1847
2. Irish Tenant League formed, 1850
3. Mass eviction, 1861
4. Isaac Butt wins by-election, 1871
5. Tenant Right meeting, 1878
6. Land War begins, 1879
7. National Land League of Mayo founded, 1879
8. John Dillon advocates boycotting, 1879
9. Irish National Land League founded, 1879
10. Captain Boycott ostracised, 1880
11. Reverend Sheehy arrested, 1881
12. Dillon & O'Brien arrested, 1886
13. United Irish League launched, 1898

# The Ulster Question

IT WAS IN 1912 that the British government, once more led by a Liberal prime minister and supported by the votes of the Irish Parliamentary Party, returned to the issue of Home Rule. The terms of the Bill introduced in April of that year were similar to earlier proposals, but provoked an even more hostile response from its opponents, particularly in Ulster.

There were several reasons why the campaign of opposition to Home Rule during 1912–14 was markedly more bitter than those of the previous generation. The Liberal Party had been shorn of its unionist wing and so a repetition of the internal divisions of 1886 was not to be expected; the veto of the House of Lords had been removed some years earlier, so a repeat of the disappointment of 1893 was impossible; and unionist support had become more concentrated in Ulster, the area of Ireland with the highest concentration of Protestants, than theretofore, when the opposition had been characterized by an all-Ireland dimension.

Led by such men as Edward Carson and James Craig, the campaign became increasingly bellicose in tone. Actions during 1912–14 such as the signing of the Solemn League and Covenant, the formation of the Ulster Volunteer Force and the Larne gun-running signalled a determination at all costs to maintain the Union intact; and when allied with other developments such as the Curragh 'mutiny' and the formation of the opposing National Volunteers, the situation in Ulster seemed to threaten the possibility of civil war.

The crisis was temporarily 'solved' by the outbreak of war in Europe in August 1914, with the Bill being passed by parliament but being suspended for the duration of hostilities. Perhaps more importantly provision was also made for the possibility of special treatment for Ulster as compared to the rest of the country. The exclusion of some or all of the nine counties of Ulster from the terms of the Bill had been bitterly opposed by nationalists, although John Redmond, leader of the Irish Parliamentary Party, had been willing to concede the principle of temporary exclusion of certain counties in order to secure the passage of the Bill as a whole. The failure adequately to resolve the objections of Ulster unionists, however, was to have fatal consequences when the question was re-examined, in even more unfavourable conditions, after the end of the war in Europe.

**The Ulster Question**

- Counties with Catholic majority, 1911 census
- Counties with Protestant majority, 1911 census
- Limit of Northern Ireland, Government of Ireland Act, 1920
- Limit of historic Ulster province

**The 1910 Election**

*Winners of parliamentary seats*

- Unionist
- Nationalist
- Independent Nationalist
- Liberal

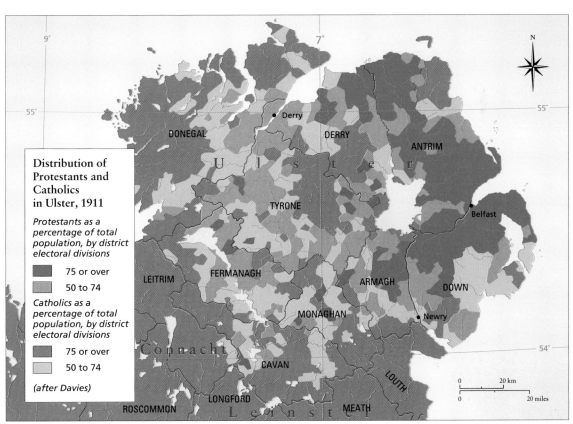

**Distribution of Protestants and Catholics in Ulster, 1911**

*Protestants as a percentage of total population, by district electoral divisions*

- 75 or over
- 50 to 74

*Catholics as a percentage of total population, by district electoral divisions*

- 75 or over
- 50 to 74

(after Davies)

# The Great War and the Easter Rising

*Above: Éamon de Valera, commander of the rebel garrison in Boland's Mills, under arrest and escorted by British troops, Dublin, 1916.*

IN COMMON with the rest of Europe the 'Great War' of 1914–18 had far-reaching consequences for Ireland. The human dimension of Ireland's contribution to the war effort was enormous, with over 270,000 men (40 per cent of the adult male population) serving in the British armed forces, and many thousands more working in the new munitions factories. The front-line soldiers were to endure the same horrifying conditions as the other combatants, and casualties also reached the same appalling levels — barely a village escaped those years without the death of at least one local young man, with particularly savage losses being inflicted at the battle of the Somme in July, 1916.

These human sufferings had a political as well as a military dimension. Many of the large numbers of nationalists who enlisted did so because they felt that their actions would serve to guarantee Home Rule for Ireland; conversely members of the Ulster Volunteer Force who volunteered felt that their sacrifices would be sufficient to ensure the defeat of the same measure. The apparent preference shown by the British government to the claims of the latter group added to the sense of discontent within the ranks of radical nationalist opinion, a discontent which was to become manifest with the events of the Easter Rising of April, 1916.

This insurrection, which lasted less than a week, was fatally hindered by poor planning, inappropriate tactics and sheer bad luck. As a consequence of divisions within the leadership of the movement the Rising, which was originally intended to encompass the entire country, was concentrated almost entirely in the centre of Dublin. In spite of the personal bravery shown by many of the insurgents, the outcome of the drama was never really in doubt and on Saturday, April 29, an unconditional surrender was signed by the leaders of the Volunteers, after a mere six days of fighting.

*Below: After the battle, citizens of Dublin walk through the rubble-strewn streets, the painful aftermath of the 1916 Easter Rising.*

In military terms the Rising was an unmitigated disaster for the Volunteers — casualties were high, with all those not killed or injured being interned by the British, and all of the munitions so painstakingly stockpiled being lost in a few short days. What the Rising did signal, however, through the actions and rhetoric of figures as diverse as Pádraig Pearse and James Connolly, was a militancy which could not be accommodated within the old Home Rule framework, and which was to become a determining factor in the Irish political scene over the next seven years.

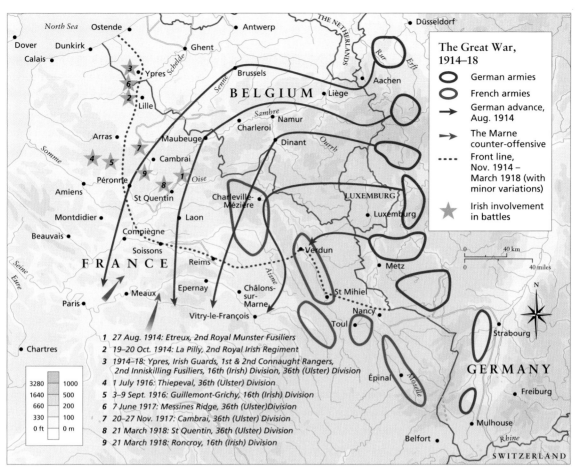

The Great War, 1914–18

- German armies
- French armies
- German advance, Aug. 1914
- The Marne counter-offensive
- Front line, Nov. 1914 – March 1918 (with minor variations)
- Irish involvement in battles

1 27 Aug. 1914: Etreux, 2nd Royal Munster Fusiliers
2 19–20 Oct. 1914: La Pilly, 2nd Royal Irish Regiment
3 1914–18: Ypres, Irish Guards, 1st & 2nd Connaught Rangers, 2nd Inniskilling Fusiliers, 16th (Irish) Division, 36th (Ulster) Division
4 1 July 1916: Thiepeval, 36th (Ulster) Division
5 3–9 Sept. 1916: Guillemont-Grichy, 16th (Irish) Division
6 7 June 1917: Messines Ridge, 36th (Ulster)Division
7 20–27 Nov. 1917: Cambrai, 36th (Ulster) Division
8 21 March 1918: St Quentin, 36th (Ulster) Division
9 21 March 1918: Roncroy, 16th (Irish) Division

Easter Rising, Dublin, 24–29 April 1916

- Rebel garrisons
- Intended British cordon
- Actual British cordon

# Separation 1916–23

Above: *King George V opening the first parliament of the new Northern Ireland on June 21, 1921.*

NATIONALIST MILITANCY was compounded by serious government errors in the aftermath of the Rising, such as the execution of the leaders of the Rising and an ill-judged proposal to introduce conscription. It gained further momentum during 1917–18, with reorganizations both of the Volunteer movement (now known as Irish Republican Army) and of Sinn Féin, which now became the main vehicle for the expression of radical nationalist sentiment. The party's sweeping victory in the 1918 General Election, where it dominated the vote outside much of Ulster, gave added momentum to the separatist effort.

This momentum was consolidated by the foundation of Dáil Eireann, a republican assembly, in January, 1919, and by the commencement in the same month of a vigorous guerrilla war undertaken by the IRA. Over the course of the next two years a number of violent incidents occurred, including 'Bloody Sunday' (marked by the deaths of twenty-three soldiers and civilians), the burning of Cork City and the destruction of the Custom House in Dublin. In an effort to stem the activities of the IRA the government introduced a number of specially-recruited and ruthlessly aggressive units into Ireland, most notoriously the so-called 'Black and Tans,' but the excesses of these units only served to diminish further the moral authority of the government in the face of world opinion. A truce between the two sides was brokered during July, 1921, following the formal partition of the country and the establishment of Northern Ireland under the Government of Ireland Act, and some months later a republican negotiating team was dispatched to London, led by Arthur Griffith and Michael Collins.

The 'Treaty' signed by this delegation with the British government in December, 1921, was unacceptable to many republicans, who felt that it did not fully recognize Ireland's legitimate claim for independence. Prominent amongst these dissenters was Éamon de Valera, who had led the underground republican Government during the War of Independence. These disagreements erupted into Civil War in June, 1922, with an attack by the Provisional Government established by the terms of the Treaty on the republican-held Four Courts in Dublin. The next twelve months saw widespread unrest, with the deaths of many leading figures on both sides, but in truth government victory was rarely in doubt. What was in doubt, however, was the ability of the new 'Irish Free State' to overcome the severe problems facing it as a young European state.

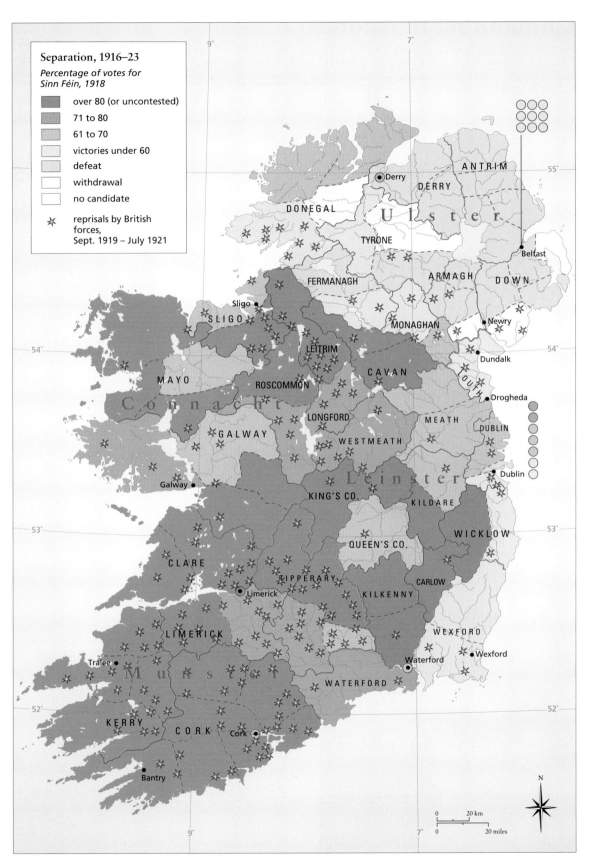

**Separation, 1916–23**

*Percentage of votes for Sinn Féin, 1918*

- over 80 (or uncontested)
- 71 to 80
- 61 to 70
- victories under 60
- defeat
- withdrawal
- no candidate

※ reprisals by British forces, Sept. 1919 – July 1921

# Cumann na nGaedheal

HAVING PREVAILED in the Civil War the Cumann na nGaedheal government, which was composed of Treaty supporters under the leadership of W.T. Cosgrave, now embarked on a comprehensive political, social and economic program designed both to promote stability and growth in the country and also to consolidate its own electoral position.

In the main the government's program was characterized by cautious continuity rather than daring innovation. In terms of the structure of the civil service, legal system, police force, army, and the education system it was content to follow the broad principles laid down by the British administration. In economic affairs continuity was also the hallmark. The government completed the process of buying out the landlords but in most other respects refused to intervene directly in the economy, although its support for the Shannon hydroelectric scheme for example demonstrated a willingness to undertake substantial projects where necessary. Ireland remained, however, a predominantly agricultural country, with most exports destined for Britain from whom she in return imported most of her manufactured goods. Taxation remained low but poverty was rife.

The government also pursued a cautious line in its foreign policy, building up a small diplomatic corps in Europe and America but concentrating on the crucial relationship with Great Britain. The issue of Northern Ireland was a persistent problem, with the border between north and south being only finally ratified in 1925, when the Boundary Commission established under the Treaty collapsed in chaos. While the government was keen to maintain good relations with the British government it also sought to consolidate its own freedom of action, and it played an important role in the Commonwealth Conferences during these years.

Internal security remained a problem, however. A potential mutiny in the Army was averted in 1924, while the defeat of the IRA in the Civil War had not removed the threat of republican sedition. De Valera was frustrated by the rather sterile abstentionist policies of Sinn Féin and founded his own party, Fianna Fáil, in 1926. In the following year he led his followers into the Free State Dáil when it appeared that the government was trying to exclude them permanently following the assassination of Kevin O'Higgins, a leading government minister.

Cumann na nGaedheal managed to hang on to power for five more years, but following the General Election of 1932 Fianna Fáil was able to form a minority government and set about implementing its radical manifesto.

*Below: William Thomas Cosgrave, President of the Irish Free State, making a speech in 1922. The new government had a dual task of rebuilding the country after the struggle for freedom and providing politically for the nation's desire for independence with unity.*

The Anti-Treaty Vote in the General Election, 1923

- - - proposed change of border

*Percentage of first-preference votes for Sinn Féin (anti-Treaty)*

| | |
|---|---|
| �in | 31 or over |
| ▦ | 21 to 30 |
| ▨ | 14 to 20 |

① January 1923: establishment of Garda training camp

② March 1924: army 'mutiny'

③ 1926: establishment of state power company

④ May 1926: public launch of Fianna Fáil

⑤ July 1927: assassination of Kevin O'Higgins

⑥ August 1927: entry of Fianna Fáil into Dáil

⑦ Establishment of state broadcasting system: 1926 Dublin, 1927 Cork, 1932 Athlone

⑧ July 1929: opening of Shannon hydroelectric scheme

⑨ 1931: IRA Wolfe Tone commemoration prohibited

# Fianna Fáil

ON COMING to power in 1932 de Valera immediately set about the task of realizing his distinctive view of national development. One of his first actions was to suspend the payment of land annuities by Irish farmers to the British overnment, which led through a series of retaliatory measures into a full-scale 'Economic War,' characterised on both sides by severe protectionist measures. De Valera seized on this opportunity to develop small domestic industries, although the damage to the agricultural sector, particularly to the small farmer group which formed the backbone of the party's rural vote, led to the gradual decline of the policy in the late 1930s.

In other areas too de Valera sought to influence Irish social development, particularly in the areas of education policy, Church-State relations and Anglo-Irish affairs. This latter issue was especially problematic, but by degrees the Cabinet succeeded in removing the most objectionable elements of the 1921 Treaty (particularly the Oath of Alliegance and the Office of Governor-General) and in 1937 de Valera successfully introduced a new Constitution.

The democratic tone of this Constitution was noteworthy at a time when fascism was at its height in Europe. Following an agreement with Great Britain in 1938, which ended the 'Economic War' and returned to Irish control several ports hitherto the responsibility of the Royal Navy, de Valera adopted a policy of military neutrality during the Second World War (or 'Emergency' as it was called in Ireland). The maintenance of this policy in spite of pressures both from the Allies (particularly after the entry of America into the War) and from Nazi Germany was a major diplomatic undertaking, one which required the government to take severe action against their former republican comrades in arms (de Valera had, in fact, immediately on coming to power, suppressed the quite distinct and quasi-fascist 'Blueshirt' movement in the country). In practice his policies favored the Allies, but his formal adherence to neutrality gained the country few friends abroad.

The government found itself increasingly unpopular after the end of the War, when a combination of continued economic hardship, the emergence of new rival political parties and a series of scandals combined to present the image of a party too long in power. Its defeat in the 1948 election, however, only served to draw attention to the momentous changes witnessed during the previous sixteen years.

**Plans for occupation of Ireland during WWII**

→ US convoys approaching British ports

---- Royal Navy patrols

⚓ treaty ports

⬛ envisaged initial German landing zone under 'Operation Green'

⬜ envisaged German advance

⬛ British troops in Northern Ireland

➤ envisaged advance of British troops under the 'W' plan

★ US naval bases

★ US air bases

☆ US army base

**Fianna Fáil**

*Percentage of first-preference votes for Fianna Fáil, 1932*

- 51 or over
- 41 to 50
- 31 to 40
- 30 or under

Northern Ireland

ANTRIM

Coleraine

Derry

DERRY

Larne

DONEGAL

Belfast

Donegal

TYRONE

DOWN

Downpatrick

FERMANAGH

ARMAGH

Enniskillen

MONAGHAN

Newry

SLIGO

Sligo

LEITRIM

CAVAN

Dundalk

LOUTH

MAYO

ROSCOMMON

LONGFORD

Drogheda

*Connacht*

MEATH

Roscommon

DUBLIN

GALWAY

WESTMEATH

Athlone

*Leinster*

Dublin

Galway

OFFALY

KILDARE

**IRISH FREE STATE**

WICKLOW

LAOIS

CLARE

TIPPERARY

Arklow

Limerick

KILKENNY

CARLOW

LIMERICK

Tipperary

WEXFORD

Tralee

Wexford

*Munster*

Waterford

WATERFORD

Youghal

KERRY

CORK

Cork

Bantry

Cobh

**Distribution of agricultural holdings, by province, 1932**

LEINSTER

MUNSTER

CONNACHT

Number of holdings in thousands

Size of holdings in acres
(0–1, 1–5, 5–15, 15–30, 30–50, 50–100, 100–200, over 200)

N

0    20 km

0    20 miles

# The '40s and '50s: Turmoil and Malaise

THE 1950s in Ireland were characterized above all by severe economic difficulties, difficulties which were exacerbated by the political instability of the period. Having only experienced two, single-party governments during the first twenty-five years of the state's existence, three short-lived governments (two 'inter-party' coalitions and one Fianna Fáil minority administration) now followed each other in quick succession. None of these cabinets was able to get to grips with the enormous problems facing the country during the period, although in 1949 the first inter-party government did take the dramatic step of formally declaring a Republic. The political scene during these years was dominated by a number of crises, most famously the 'Mother and Child' debacle of 1951, when a proposal to reform the health care provided to expectant mothers and young children collapsed amidst political indecision and pressure from the Catholic Church and the medical profession.

Such a political situation provided a decidedly unhelpful context in which to address the enormous economic problems facing the country. Foremost amongst these was a resurgence in emigration, which reached levels not witnessed since the 1880s and which came to symbolize the failure of the Irish state to provide a basic standard of living for its citizens, contrary to the hopes and expectations of those who had campaigned so hard for its independence. This increase in emigrants was due to a combination of factors, most notably the increasing use of machinery in rural areas which reduced the demand for farm labor, the lack of indigenous industrial development in urban centers and the enormous demand for labor in the major industrial centers in Britain. All these factors conspired to siphon off enormous numbers of young Irish men and women, with the poverty-stricken areas of the western seaboard being particularly badly affected.

While some efforts were made to arrest this loss of population, which was accentuated by a decline in the marriage rate, there was little scope for innovative policy given the restrictions imposed by the prevailing economic orthodoxies. It was only with the election in 1959 of Seán Lemass as Taoiseach and leader of Fianna Fáil in succession to de Valera (who was subsequently elected to two terms as President of Ireland) that the almost hermetically-sealed nature of the Irish economy and society was finally opened up to external influences.

**Death rate from Tuberculosis, 1950–54**

- Increase
- Decrease up to 30%
- Decrease from 31 to 60%
- Decrease over 60%

DONEGAL

Northern Ireland
Subject to U.K. National
Health organization
founded 1946

MONAGHAN

SLIGO
LEITRIM
CAVAN
MAYO
ROSCOMMON
LOUTH
Connacht
LONGFORD
MEATH
WESTMEATH
DUBLIN
GALWAY
Leinster
OFFALY
KILDARE

LAOIS
WICKLOW
CLARE
CARLOW
TIPPERARY
KILKENNY
LIMERICK
WEXFORD
Munster
KERRY
WATERFORD
CORK

N

0      40 km
0            40 miles

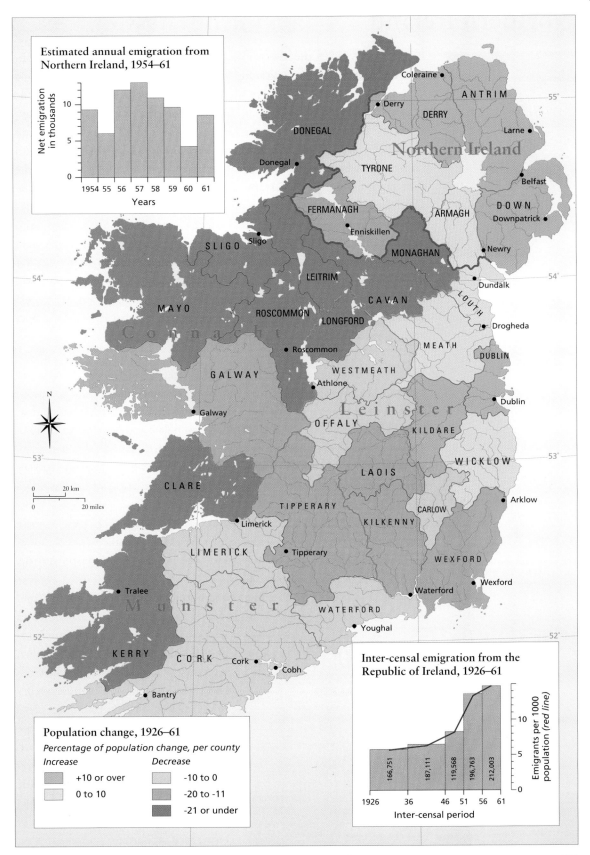

Estimated annual emigration from
Northern Ireland, 1954–61

Net emigration
in thousands

1954 55 56 57 58 59 60 61
Years

DONEGAL

Coleraine
Derry
DERRY
ANTRIM
Larne
Northern Ireland

Donegal
TYRONE

Belfast

FERMANAGH
ARMAGH
DOWN
Downpatrick

Enniskillen

MONAGHAN

Newry

SLIGO
Sligo

LEITRIM
Dundalk

CAVAN
LOUTH

Connacht

MAYO
ROSCOMMON
LONGFORD
Drogheda

Roscommon
MEATH

WESTMEATH
DUBLIN

GALWAY
Athlone

Galway
Leinster
Dublin

OFFALY
KILDARE

WICKLOW

N

LAOIS

0    20 km
0    20 miles

CLARE
TIPPERARY
CARLOW
Arklow

KILKENNY

Limerick

LIMERICK
Tipperary
WEXFORD

Tralee
Wexford

Munster
Waterford

WATERFORD

Youghal

KERRY
CORK
Cork

Cobh

Bantry

Population change, 1926–61
*Percentage of population change, per county*
*Increase*                    *Decrease*

| | |
|---|---|
| +10 or over | -10 to 0 |
| 0 to 10 | -20 to -11 |
| | -21 or under |

Inter-censal emigration from the
Republic of Ireland, 1926–61

Emigrants per 1000
population (*red line*)

166,751    187,111    119,568    196,763    212,003

1926    36    46    51    56    61
Inter-censal period

# Northern Ireland

Above: *James Craig, Lord Craigavon, the first Prime Minister of Northern Ireland.*

BY THE LATE 1950S the six-county 'statelet' of Northern Ireland, established under the 1920 Government of Ireland Act, had also performed very badly in terms of social and economic development. One of the reasons for this stagnation was the nature of the original political settlement. Born out of Unionist opposition both to Home Rule and republican separatism, the territory encompassed by the state was a compromise between the historic nine-county province of Ulster and the four counties where Protestants enjoyed numerical superiority over the Catholic community. The presence of substantial Catholic communities in border areas presented the new government (led by Sir James Craig) with severe difficulties, particularly during the years 1922–23 which were marked by severe communal violence. The confirmation of the border in 1925, by means of a tripartite agreement with the Free State and British cabinets (in return for which Dublin received financial concessions), meant that the Unionist government in Belfast was free to turn its attention to the consolidation of state and party interests.

Almost immediately complaints began to emerge regarding the abuse of the rights of the Catholic/nationalist minority. These complaints were concentrated in particular on electoral arrangements, which, it was suggested, were manipulated in the interests of the Unionist Party; on public and private employment, which Catholics alleged was characterized by severe religious discrimination; on security arrangements, which seemed at times geared more towards the suppression of political dissent rather than criminal activity; and on education, where, for a number of reasons Catholic schools received less financial assistance than their state-sponsored Protestant counterparts. While some of these grievances may have been exaggerated it seems clear that the political aspirations of the general Catholic community were regarded with hostility at the highest levels of the Northern state.

The decision of the Stormont government to participate in the Second World War drove a further wedge between it and neutral Éire. The experience of wartime industrial and military mobilization, and the tragedy of the Belfast Blitz, inevitably placed an emotional distance between north and south, a distance confirmed by the 1949 Ireland Act, which guaranteed the maintenance of the state so long as it enjoyed majority support. Notwithstanding the poor economic performance of the 1950s there seemed little danger that the government, now headed by Sir Basil Brooke, was in any danger of losing such support.

Below: *Inter-communal violence has a long and depressing history in Northern Ireland. This newspaper headline dates from 1935, at which time the tradition of civil unrest was already almost a century old.*

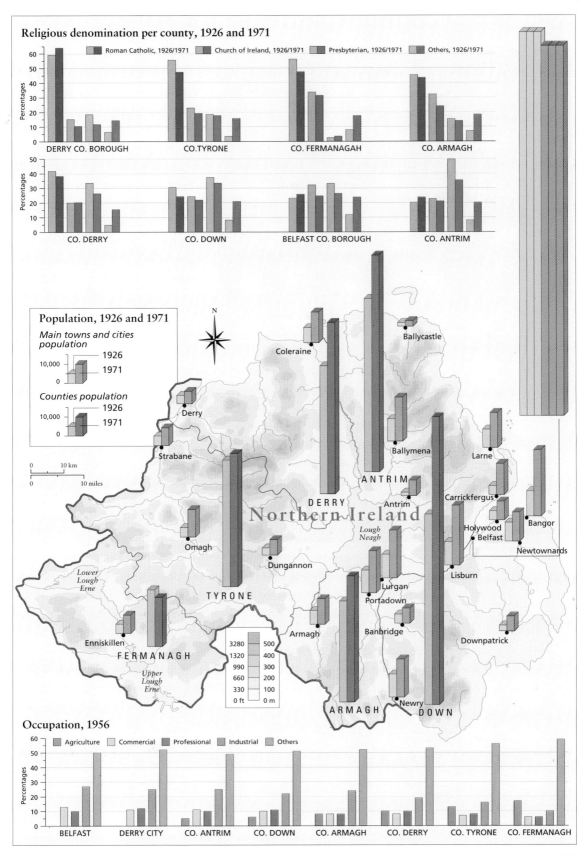

## Religious denomination per county, 1926 and 1971

Roman Catholic, 1926/1971 ■ Church of Ireland, 1926/1971 ■ Presbyterian, 1926/1971 ■ Others, 1926/1971

DERRY CO. BOROUGH  CO.TYRONE  CO. FERMANAGAH  CO. ARMAGH

CO. DERRY  CO. DOWN  BELFAST CO. BOROUGH  CO. ANTRIM

## Population, 1926 and 1971

*Main towns and cities population*

10,000 — 1926 / 1971

*Counties population*

10,000 — 1926 / 1971

0 — 10 km
0 — 10 miles

N

Coleraine
Ballycastle
Derry
Strabane
Ballymena
Larne
ANTRIM
Carrickfergus
DERRY
Antrim
Holywood
Bangor
Omagh
Lough Neagh
Belfast
Newtownards
Dungannon
Northern Ireland
Lisburn
Lower Lough Erne
Lurgan
TYRONE
Portadown
Armagh
Banbridge
Enniskillen
Downpatrick
FERMANAGH
Upper Lough Erne
Newry
ARMAGH  DOWN

3280 / 500
1320 / 400
990 / 300
660 / 200
330 / 100
0 ft / 0 m

## Occupation, 1956

■ Agriculture ■ Commercial ■ Professional ■ Industrial ■ Others

BELFAST  DERRY CITY  CO. ANTRIM  CO. DOWN  CO. ARMAGH  CO. DERRY  CO. TYRONE  CO. FERMANAGH

# The '60s: Economic and Social Change

Above: *Jack Lynch (Taoiseach 1966–73, 1977–79) signing the treaty of accession to the European Economic Community on behalf of the Republic of Ireland in 1973.*

A MAJOR DEPARTURE in economic policy in the Republic occurred with the publication in 1958 of the Program for Economic Expansion. This report (which was followed by two more ambitious programs) advocated the abandonment of self-sufficiency in favor of an economic policy based on free trade, with the emphasis now on increased exports and the attraction of foreign investment into Ireland.

In economic terms the new policy proved very successful, with output and employment reaching levels never before recorded in the history of the state, although both small farmers and those employed in the old 'protected' industries did not share equally in the new prosperity. Emigration fell and a substantial number of those who had left in the 1950s now returned to the country. People started to marry at an earlier age than theretofore, and the birth rate began to fall.

Not surprisingly these economic and demographic changes heralded new patterns of social development. Perhaps the most important was the establishment in 1961 of a national television station, Radio Telefís Éireann, which provided a forum for social and political debate hitherto rather lacking. Evidence of new thinking was also evident in religious practice building on the deliberations of the Second Vatican Council; in educational policy, with the introduction of free secondary education; in the area of gender relations, with new opportunities opening up for Irish women; in the field of popular culture, with exposure to new styles of music, literature and art, frequently imported from Britain and America and less subject to stultifying censorship; and in the party political field, with a new emphasis upon technocratic management at the expense of old-style nationalist rhetoric.

Not everything had changed, however, and not all change was progressive: the new materialist ethos inevitably meant that those on the margins of Irish society could not fully share in the new-found wealth. Many of the 'gains' of the period proved rather ephemeral, particularly when the international economic climate turned sour in the 1970s. That said, the 1960s were characterized by a social dynamic, which, while not revolutionary, was certainly a welcome change from the atrophied atmosphere of the 1950s. The decision to enter the EEC, overwhelmingly endorsed by popular referendum in 1973, seemed to symbolize this new era although such support was undoubtedly more the result of rational economic self-interest than any new-found interest in wider European affairs.

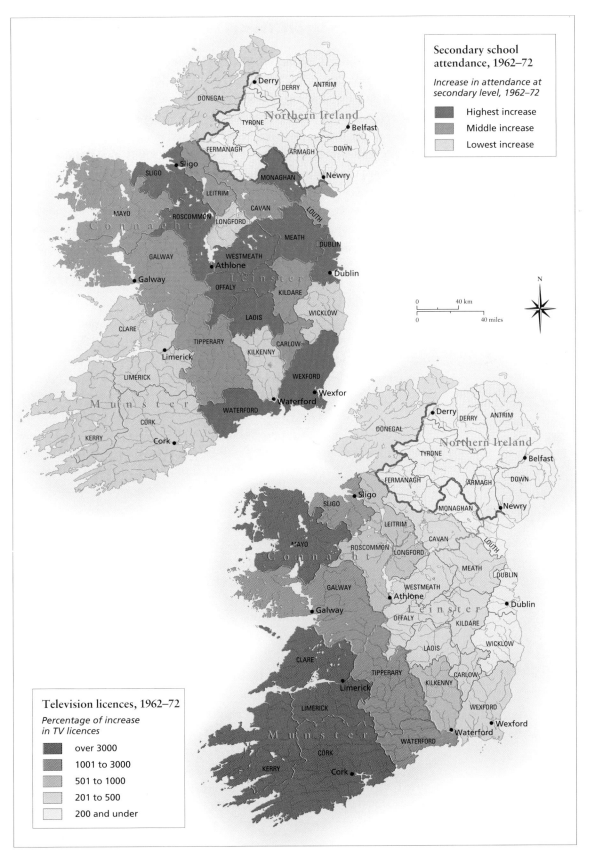

Secondary school attendance, 1962–72

*Increase in attendance at secondary level, 1962–72*

- Highest increase
- Middle increase
- Lowest increase

Television licences, 1962–72

*Percentage of increase in TV licences*

- over 3000
- 1001 to 3000
- 501 to 1000
- 201 to 500
- 200 and under

# The '70s and '80s: Political and Social Instability

The expansionist economic policy heralded by the First Economic Program was dependent on a benign international trading environment, and for most of the next fifteen years such was indeed the case. When this basis was destroyed by the 'stagflation' (high inflation accompanied by increasing unemployment) which afflicted most developed economies following the oil-price rise of 1973, the country was plunged once more into severe economic difficulties. Over the next fifteen years, through a combination of a series of international depressions, massive government borrowing, and a decline in the financial assistance forthcoming from the European Community (which affected rural areas particularly badly) the country experienced economic turmoil which threatened to undermine the progress made in the 1960s.

Such instability was evident in the political as well as the economic field. Having experienced fifteen years of uninterrupted Fianna Fáil government between 1958 and 1973 the country now experienced a series of coalitions and short-term minority administrations (with the exception of the landslide Fianna Fáil victory of 1977, which was to be tarnished within two years by a series of internal disputes), with seven General Elections being held between 1973 and 1989.

The 1980s also witnessed a new style of political debate in the country, focused in particular on the provisions of the 1937 Constitution and which saw bitterly-contested referenda in 1983 (on the issue of abortion) and 1986 (on the issue of divorce). A host of new political issues also came to the fore, particularly with regard to the quality of the environment and the provision of local services. Few administrations devised satisfactory long-term solutions to these thorny problems, and a resurgence in emigration in the late 1980s bore eloquent testimony to the sense of crisis within the Irish body politic.

It was not all doom and gloom, however, and a number of developments in the sporting and cultural fields highlighted the latent potential beneath the political stalemate. The international acclaim earned by a series of Irish authors, playwrights and musicians was mirrored by a number of sporting successes, perhaps most notably the achievements of the national football team in reaching the finals of the European Championships in Germany in 1988 and the World Cup in Italy in 1990, events which gave rise to massive, spontaneous outpourings of national pride.

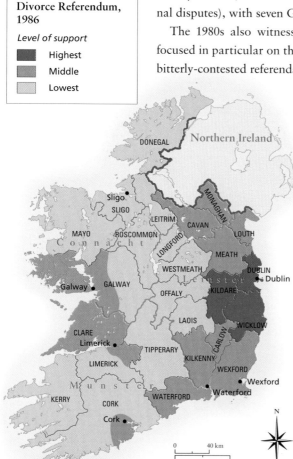

**Divorce Referendum, 1986**

*Level of support*

- Highest
- Middle
- Lowest

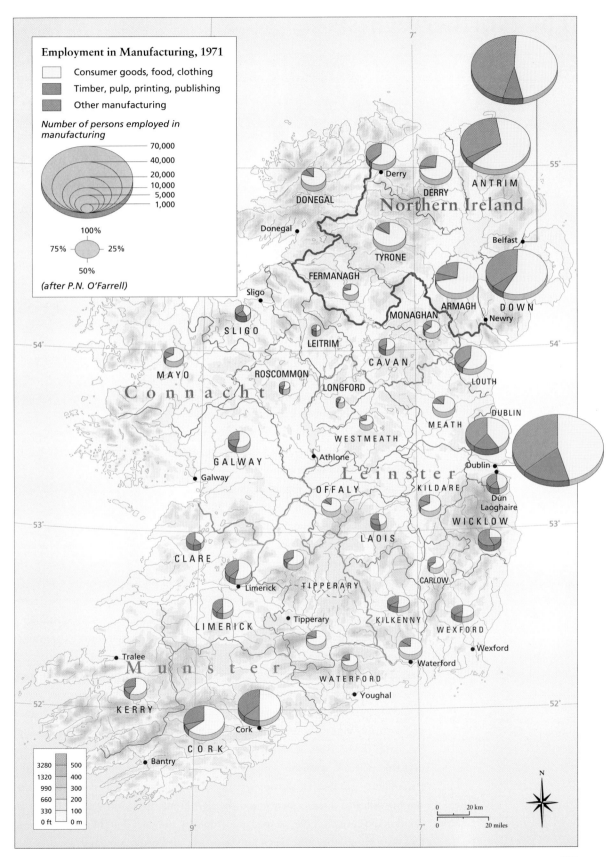

## Employment in Manufacturing, 1971

Consumer goods, food, clothing

Timber, pulp, printing, publishing

Other manufacturing

*Number of persons employed in manufacturing*

70,000
40,000
20,000
10,000
5,000
1,000

100%
75%    25%
50%

*(after P.N. O'Farrell)*

Derry

DONEGAL

Donegal

DERRY

Northern Ireland

ANTRIM

55°

Belfast

TYRONE

FERMANAGH

Sligo

MONAGHAN

ARMAGH

DOWN

Newry

SLIGO

LEITRIM

54°

CAVAN

LOUTH

54°

MAYO

ROSCOMMON

LONGFORD

MEATH

Connacht

WESTMEATH

DUBLIN

Athlone

Leinster

Dublin

GALWAY

OFFALY

KILDARE

Galway

Dún
Laoghaire

53°

LAOIS

WICKLOW

53°

CLARE

TIPPERARY

CARLOW

Limerick

LIMERICK

Tipperary

KILKENNY

WEXFORD

Wexford

Tralee

Munster

Waterford

Youghal

52°

KERRY

WATERFORD

52°

Cork

CORK

Bantry

N

3280    500
1320    400
990     300
660     200
330     100
0 ft    0 m

0        20 km

0        20 miles

# The Northern Crisis

*Above: Margaret Thatcher and Garret FitzGerald, whose governments negotiated the Anglo-Irish Agreement of 1985 which gave Dublin an input into the affairs of Northern Ireland, much to the fury of unionists.*

THE 1960s were a decade of frustrated hope for Northern Ireland. Beginning with the promise of a new era based on improved economic performance and greater harmony between the Catholic and Protestant communities, these policies, associated with Captain Terence O'Neill, who was appointed Prime Minister in 1963, foundered on the rocks of social and political intransigence.

The frequent confrontations between Catholic Civil Rights demonstrators and Protestant opponents produced an increasingly tense atmosphere which erupted into open communal violence in 1969, in which year the British Army was deployed in Northern Ireland in an effort to restore calm.

Unfortunately, as a consequence of such misjudged policies as the Falls Road curfew and internment without trial, the opposite occurred and the six counties experienced a spiral of violence which culminated in 1972 with an orgy of shootings and bombings unparalleled since the violence of 1922–23. Particularly prominent in these disturbances was a number of paramilitary groupings, most notably the Provisional IRA (an extreme republican organization) and the Ulster Defence Association (an equally ruthless loyalist force).

In an effort to deal with the deteriorating situation the British government prorogued Stormont and commenced 'direct rule' from Westminster. A series of initiatives followed—the Sunningdale Agreement (1973), the Power Sharing Executive (1974), the 'Rolling Devolution' plan of the early 1980s—each of which acknowledged the complexity of the situation but none of which could command cross-community support. The Anglo-Irish Agreement of 1985 institutionalized the recognition accorded by the British government to the legitimate interest of the Irish government in Northern Ireland, but notwithstanding such intermittent progress the violence associated with the unrest continued, with deaths from 'the Troubles' eventually exceeding 3,000.

A glimmer of light emerged in the late 1980s when provisional talks were arranged between the major parties as part of the 'three-strand' process, which acknowledged the three principal elements of the problem—the internal divisions in Northern Ireland, the relationship between the north and south of Ireland, and the issue of British/Irish relations. A major breakthrough appeared to have occurred in 1994, with the calling of ceasefires by both republican and loyalist paramilitary groups, but the opportunity was lost as a consequence of time-consuming political disagreements, and the IRA bomb attack on Canary Wharf in London in February, 1996, seemed unfortunately to signal that the 'peace process' had been yet another false dawn for the people of Northern Ireland.

## The Northern Crisis

1. October 1968: Civil Rights march conflicts with police
2. January 1969: march attacked
3. August 1969: British troops deployed
4. July 1970: Falls Road curfew
5. August 1971: Internment swoop
6. January 1972: 'Bloody Sunday'
7. July 1972: 'Bloody Friday'
8. May 1974: Car bomb
9. January 1976: 10 workmen shot dead
10. August 1976: Peace People movement starts
11. 1978: 'Dirty protest' by prisoners
12. August 1979: 18 paratroopers killed in explosion
13. August 1979: Lord Mountbatten assassinated
14. 1980–81: hunger strikes
15. 1982: 17 people killed in bombing
16. November 1985: Anglo-Irish Agreement signed
17. May 1987: 8 IRA members shot
18. November 1987: 11 killed at War Memorial bombing
19. January 1992: 8 killed in IRA bombing
20. October 1993: Shankill Road bombing
21. October 1993: Grey Steel shootings by Loyalists
22. 1995–97: Orangemen maech on Drumcree

## Seats Won at the General Election, 1997

- United Kingdom Unionist
- Ulster Unionist Party
- Social Democratic and Labour Party
- Democratic Unionist Party
- Sinn Féin

# Ireland in the '90s

IT IS FAIR to say that Ireland in the 1990s is a more complex and rapidly-changing society than at any time in its recent history. Evidence of change abounds—the population is one of the most youthful in Europe, new industries are daily established, old forms of religious faith and practice are coming under sustained pressure. Such social change is also evident at the political level, with the emergence of a new cross-party economic consensus and a blurring of the traditional party lines derived from the Civil War period. Perhaps no other event better highlights this process of change than the election in 1990 of Mary Robinson as President of Ireland. Female, an avowed liberal, youthful—she personified the challenge to the inherited patterns of power and authority in the country, and while she was circumscribed by the nature of her office from engaging directly in the debates about the nation's future yet her very presence in Áras an Uachtaráin became a symbol of the potency of the ideas she espoused.

But while evidence of change is to be seen in abundance yet even amidst such contemporary dynamism there are still powerful echoes of the nation's past. Perhaps the most graphic of these images come from Northern Ireland, where the manifold tragedies of political violence and sectarian division continue to present a vivid tapestry of human suffering. But there are other, more subtle and engaging expressions of continuity—the influential position occupied by agriculture in the national economy, the vibrancy of traditional forms of sport and culture, the impulse towards a satisfactory definition of nationality—in these and myriad other forms historic Ireland continues to exercise a degree of influence over the direction in which modern Irish society is moving. It seems reasonable to suggest that this tension between continuity and change, between fidelity to tradition and the accommodation of innovation, will continue to be a hallmark of the Irish experience of future generations as it has been of the past.

Below: *Mary Robinson's surprise success in the 1990 presidential elections broke the mold. A champion of women's rights, a left-of-center social progressive, her victory shook the conservative, male-dominated, religious and Republican hold on Irish politics.*

**Dáil elections, 1997 (proportional representation)**

□ 1 seat won

Progressive Democrats
Fianna Fáil
Labour
Fine Gael
Democratic Left
Greens
Workers Party
Sinn Féin
Others

**New Composition of Dáil Éireann**

45.4 Percentage of seats
(77) Number of seats

46.4 (77)
32.5 (54)
10.8 (18)
4.2 (7)
1.8 (3)
2.4 (4)
1.2 (2)
0.6 (1)

NATIONAL

39.3
27.9
10.4
9.4
6.6
2.6
2.8
2.5
0.4 (Wp)

**Distribution of votes, by percentage**

DUBLIN CITY AND COUNTY

36.4
22.4
11.2
9.4
6.6
5.7
5
2.6
0.7

REST OF LEINSTER

40.4
29.4
14.4
5.3
4.4
1.3
2.2
2.4

CONNACHT - ULSTER

43
33
9.5
5.2
5
3.2
1.1

MUNSTER

38.6
28.2
12.5
10.1
4.2
1.7
0.8
1.8
2.1

# Chronology

8,000 BC    First people arrive in Ireland, perhaps across the land bridge from Scotland.

3,000 BC    Arrival of New Stone Age people who built Newgrange.

c. 200 BC    Arrival of speakers of what develops into Gaelic.

AD 78–84    Roman Governor of Britain, Agricola, considers the invasion and conquest of Ireland.

c. 130–80    Ptolemy's account of Ireland.

367    Major offensive on Britain by the Irish, Picts and Saxons.

431    Pope sends Palladius as bishop to Irish Christians.

432    St. Patrick arrives to help convert pagan Gaelic kings to Christianity (traditional date).

c. 550–650    The growth of monasticism in Ireland.

563    Foundation of Iona by Columba.

575    Convention of Druim Ceat.

7th and 8th centuries    Ireland's Golden Age, *Book of Durrow, Book of Kells,* Ardagh Chalice.

c. 670–700    Tírechán and Muirchú produce hagiographical works on St. Patrick.

697    Synod of Birr and the proclamation of the 'Law of the Innocents'.

c. 700    The Eóganacht become dominant in Munster.

721–42    Cathal mac Finguine King of Munster.

c. 725    Uí Briúm dynasty gain dominance in Connacht.

734    Abduction of Flaithbertach mac Loingsig. Cenél Conaill now excluded from Uí Néill overkingship.

743    Clann Cholmáin first take the overkingship of Uí Néill.

795    First Viking raid on Iona, Rathlin, Inishmurray and Inishbofin.

806    Vikings murder sixty eight members of Iona community.

820–47    Feidlimid MacCrimthainn King of Munster.

836    Viking raids penetrate deep inland.

837–42    Large Vikings fleets appear and overwinter on the Boyne, the Liffey, Lough Neagh and in Dublin.

842    First reported Viking-Irish alliance.

845    Abbot of Armagh captured by Vikings.

846–62    The reign of Máel Sechnaill I, powerful Overking of Uí Néill.

914    The Second wave of Viking raids.

980    Máel Sechnaill II becomes Overking of Uí Néill.

975–1014    Brian Boru King of Munster.

997    Brian Boru and Máel Sechnaill II divide Ireland.

999    Brian Boru defeats the Leinstermen and the Ostmen at Glenn Máma. Sitric Silkenbeard, King of Dublin, surrenders.

1002–14    Brian Boru King of Ireland.

1014    Death of Brian Boru at the Battle of Clontarf.

1142    Foundation of the first Cistercian house in Ireland.

1169    Arrival of English military leaders, FitzStephen, FitzGerald and others.

1170–71    Arrival of 'Strongbow' in person. Strongbow becomes King of Leinster. Arrival of Henry II. Submission of most Irish bishops and Irish Kings.

1175    Treaty of Windsor between Henry II and Rory O'Connor High King of Ireland, who submits to rule unoccupied regions as a vassal.

1176    Death of Strongbow.

1177    Prince John made Lord of Ireland—first visit 1185.

c. 1200    Start of Classical Irish period in literature, lasting until 1600.

1210    King John's second visit. Confiscation of the Earldom of Ulster and Honor of Limerick—submission of some Irish kings.

1260    Battle of Down, death of Brian O'Neill.

1261    Battle of Callan.

1315    Invasion of Ireland by Edward Bruce. Proclaimed by Irish allies as King of Ireland.

1316    Rebellious Irish Chiefs defeated at Athenry.

1318    Battle of Dysert O'Dea. Battle of Faughart, Edward Bruce killed.

1333    Murder of Earl of Ulster, William de Burgh. Crown looses control of Anglo-Norman Connacht and the Irish Chiefs in Ulster.

1366    Statutes of Kilkenny to try and prevent English settlers adopting the Irish language1394–95 King Richard II's first expedition to Ireland.

1414–47    Continual feud between political groupings of James Butler, fourth Earl of Ormond and John Talbot Earl of Shrewsbury, for control of Royal government of Ireland.

1494    In the wake of Anglo-Irish support for Perkin Warbeck, Henry VII dismisses Kildare in 1492. Lord Deputy, Sir Edward Poynings, establishes 'Poynings Law' making all English parliamentary legislation applicable to Ireland.

1496    Kildare reappointed.

1504    Battle of Knockaoe. Kildare victorious.

1509    Accession of Henry VIII.

| | |
|---|---|
| 1515 | Anarchy sweeps Ireland. |
| 1534 | The Kildare Rebellion leads to Kildare's arrest and death. Lord Offaly takes leadership of revolt. |
| 1536 | Fall of Maynooth Castle—arrest of Lord Offaly and five uncles (all brought to England). |
| 1536–37 | Meeting of the Irish Reformation Parliament. |
| 1540 | Sir Anthony St. Leger becomes Governor of Ireland. |
| 1541 | A Parliamentary meeting declares Henry VIII King of Ireland. The establishing of the 'Surrender and Re-grant' program. |
| 1558 | Accession of Elizabeth I following the death of Mary I. The strong state support Reformation unpopular in Ireland. |
| 1565–71 | Sir Henry Sidney governor of Ireland. |
| 1569–71 | Parliament declares the Lordship of Tyrone under the power of the Crown, thus leading to revolts in Munster, Leinster and Connacht against the policy. |
| 1571–75 | Sir William FitzWilliam Governor of Ireland. |
| 1573 | Private Colonization ventures continue in Ulster. |
| 1576 | Reappointed Sidney launches conciliatory policy halting any further private colonization. |
| 1579–80 | Rebellion in Munster. Exacerbated by a second revolt in Leinster led by James Eustace, Viscount Baltinglas and Feagh Mac Hugh O'Byrne. Support from discontented Palesmen. Arthur Lord Grey de Wilton is given the position of Governor to deal with the 'dual revolt'. Defeated at Glenmalure in Wicklow but success at Smerwick. |
| 1582–83 | The suppression of both revolts at Munster and Leinster culminates in the killing of Earl of Desmond. |
| 1595 | Rebellion of Hugh O'Neill, Earl of Tyrone. |
| 1598 | O'Neill victorious at Yellow Ford, Ulster. |
| 1601 | O'Donnell, O'Neill and Spaniards defeated by Mountjoy at the Battle of Kinsale. |
| 1603 | The assession of James I leads to the enforcement of English Law in Ireland, especially Ulster. Hugh O'Neill and Earl of Tyrone surrender. |
| 1607 | The 'Flight of the Earls', O'Neill, Earl of Tyrone, O'Donnell, Earl of Tyrconnell. |
| 1608 | Plantation of Derry (City of London). Six other confiscated counties planned. |
| 1641 | Great Catholic-Gaelic rebellion for return of lands. Ireland thrown into chaos. |
| 1642 | Irish suppression hoped for by English Parliament with the 'Adventurers Act'. Robert Munro and army land in Ulster in April. Civil War in England. Catholic Confederation assembles at Kilkenny. |

| | |
|---|---|
| 1649 | Execution of Charles I. Cromwell's arrival in Ireland leads to capture of Drogheda, Wexford, New Ross. There follows a Cromwellian conquest and subsequent implementation of plantations. |
| 1658 | Death of Cromwell. |
| 1660 | Restoration period—accession of Charles II. Uphold Cromwellian conquest but restore property to 'innocent papists.' |
| 1665 | 'Act of Explanation' obliges grantees of Cromwell to surrender one third of their lands to 'innocents.' |
| 1685 | Accession of James II. |
| 1686–87 | The newly appointed Earl of Tyrconnell, Richard Talbot, replaces Protestant officials with Catholics. |
| 1688 | Deposition of James II in England. Gates of Derry closed to James' troops. |
| 1695 | Fourteen per cent of Irish land held by Catholics. Rights of Catholics restricted in education, arms-bearing, horse owning and the Catholic clergy banished. |
| 1699 | Acts restricting Irish woollen exports. |
| 1704 | Catholics' presence restricted in landholding and public offices. |
| 1713 | Jonathan Swift becomes Dean of St. Patrick's. |
| 1728 | Act removing franchise from Catholics. |
| 1741 | First performance of Handel's *Messiah* in Fishamble Street Music Hall. |
| 1775 | Henry Grattan leader of Patriot Party. |
| 1782 | Irish Parliament successful in gaining 'legislative independence' from British. |
| 1791 | Wolfe Tone's *Argument on behalf of the Catholics of Ireland*. Leads to foundation of Society of United Irishmen. |
| 1792 | Relief Act allows Catholics to practice law. |
| 1796–98 | United Irishmen plotting rebellion. Rebellion in Wexford in May. Humbert lands in Killala in August. Tone arrested and dies in November. |
| 1800 | Act of Union—Ireland governed henceforth by Westminster. |
| 1803 | Robert Emmet's rising, trial and execution. |
| 1822 | Irish Constabulary Act (establishing county police forces and a salaried magistracy). |
| 1823 | Catholic Association founded, led by Daniel O'Connell. |
| 1828 | O'Connell elected for County Clare. |
| 1829 | Catholic Emancipation passed. |
| 1837 | Accession of Queen Victoria. |

1840    O'Connell's Repeal Association founded.

1842    *The Nation* newspaper founded by Thomas Davis.

1843    O'Connell's 'Monster Meetings' for Repeal of the Union.

1845    Blight in the potato harvest. Beginning of Great Famine (1845–49).

1846    Repeal of Corn Laws. August sees Public Works started but stopped due to expectation of new harvest. Total failure of potato harvest. Public Works restarted. October sees first deaths from starvation.

1847    Foundation of Irish Confederation. Free rations first handed out from Government soup kitchens, thus leading to distress thrown on localities.

1848–49    Worst years of Great Famine. Rebellion by Young Ireland movement. Battle of the Widow MacCormack's Cabbage Garden at Ballingarry.

1858    After James Stephens returns from France he establishes the Irish Republican Brotherhood. Fenian Brotherhood founded in the U.S.A.

1861    Beginning of American Civil War.

1866    Archbishop Paul Cullen becomes the first Irish Cardinal.

1867    Attempted Fenian rising.

1869    Disestablishment of the Church of Ireland by W.E. Gladstone.

1870    Gladstone's first Land Act recognizing tenant's right (August) and the foundation of Home Government Association by Isaac Butt (September).

1875    Charles Stewart Parnell elected MP for County Meath.

1879    Threat of famine in Ireland. Irish National Land League founded, instigated by Michael Davitt, widespread evictions.

1879–82    Land War.

1881    Gladstone's second Land Act.

1891    Parnell marries Katharine O'Shea (June), dies at Brighton (October).

1893    Second Home Rule Bill. Gaelic League founded.

1898    United Irish League founded.

1900    John Redmond elected chairman of Irish Parliamentary Party and United Irish League.

1907    Dockers' strike and riots in Belfast.

1914    Illegal importation of arms by Ulster Volunteers and Irish Volunteers. Buckingham Palace conference collapses just before outbreak of World War I.

1915    Reorganization of the Irish Republican Brotherhood and formation of military council formation (December).

1916    Irish Republic proclaimed in Dublin (April 24). There follows martial law, rebel surrender, imprisonments and 15 executions. The Ulster Division also loses significant numbers in the Battle of the Somme.

1917    The Irish Convention ineffectual and Sinn Féin and Irish Volunteers reorganize.

1918    The General Election sees Republican success and the formation of Dáil Éireann in following January.

1920    The Government of Ireland Act introduces partition between two Home Rule states. Dublin's 'Bloody Sunday'.

1921    IRA setback. King opens Northern Ireland Parliament in Belfast. Sir James Craig Prime Minister in Northern Ireland. A truce is called. December witnesses Anglo-Irish Treaty.

1922    Convention of Anti-Treaty IRA. 'Special' powers given to Northern Ireland police. National Army given emergency powers after murder of Collins. Irish Free State established, Northern Ireland excluded.

1923    End of Civil War—IRA 'dump arms.' Free State admitted to League of Nations.

1924    National Army re-organization, cutbacks and mutiny.

1925    Partition confirmed by tripartite agreement.

1926    De Valera founds Fianna Fáil. General election in Free State.

1929    Proportional representation abolished in Northern Ireland.

1930    Irish Labour Party and TU Congress separate.

1931    Banning of the IRA in Free State.

1932    In the general election Fianna Fáil prove successful.

1933    National Guard (Blueshirts) formed. United Ireland Party (Fine Gael) formed under O'Duffy (Blueshirts leader).

1934    Cosgrave reinstated as O'Duffy resigns.

1935    Importation and sale of contraceptives banned in Free State.

1936    Free State Senate abolished.

1937    Constitution of Éire replaces Free State.

1938    UK agree to subsidise Northern Ireland Social Welfare payments to UK standards.

1939    IRA bombing campaign on Great Britain in World War II. Éire neutral.

| | |
|---|---|
| 1940 | Death of IRA hunger strikers in Éire. Anglo-Irish military consultations. Economic sanctions imposed on Éire. |
| 1941 | The most destructive German air raids on Belfast and Dublin. Death of James Joyce. |
| 1945 | Congress of Irish Unions formed after split in Trade Union Congress. Churchill's and de Valera's radio speeches post-World War II. |
| 1946 | Northern Ireland National Insurance in align with Great Britain. |
| 1948 | NHS introduced in Northern Ireland—Irish Republic enacted after Costello's repeal of External Relations Act. Fianna Fáil lose election, de Valera out of office after sixteen years. |
| 1949 | Ireland Act, agreement that partition will be perpetuated. |
| 1954 | IRA attacks in Armagh. |
| 1955 | Republic admitted to UNO. |
| 1956–62 | Border campaign initiated by IRA. |
| 1958 | First program for economic growth in the Republic. |
| 1961 | Republic unsuccessful in joining EEC. |
| 1964 | Lemass-O'Neill talks held on reconciliation. |
| 1966 | Anglo-Irish Free Trade Agreement. |
| 1967 | NI Civil Rights Association founded. |
| 1968 | First Civil Rights march. Clash in Derry between CRA and police. O'Neill's program for the removal of discrimination of Catholics in local government, housing and franchise. |
| 1969 | People's Democracy march from Belfast to Derry in January. There follows a series of explosions. Chichester Clark becomes Prime Minister. British troops sent in. |
| 1970 | Dublin Arms Trial. Splits in Sinn Féin and IRA lead to provisional factions setting up. |
| 1971 | Paisley's Democratic Unionist Party founded. Re-introduction of internment. First British soldier killed by IRA in Belfast. |
| 1972 | Following Derry's Bloody Sunday in January, Direct Rule is imposed. |
| 1973 | Republic, UK and NI join EEC. Proportional representation restored in NI (December). Sunningdale Agreement. |
| 1974 | Multiple deaths in Dublin bombing. Guildford and Birmingham pub bombings in Nov. and Dec. |
| 1975 | NI internment suspended. |
| 1976 | British ambassador in Dublin killed. Republic's Emergency Powers Bill referred to Supreme Court by President. |
| 1978 | Twelve killed by Provisionals' fire bombs in a County Down restaurant. |
| 1979 | Earl Mountbatten and relations killed in County Sligo. Eighteen soldiers killed at Warrenpoint, County Down. Relaxation of Republic's ban on contraceptives. |
| 1979 | Visit of Pope John Paul II. |
| 1981 | Following the death of Republican hunger-strikers, the Provisionals' strategy of 'H-block' protests collapses. |
| 1982 | Mass killings of soldiers at Knightsbridge (July) and Ballykelly, County Derry, (December). |
| 1983 | Referendum bans abortion in Republic. |
| 1985 | Bitter Protestant disagreement over Anglo-Irish Agreement at Hillsborough. |
| 1986 | Confirmation of Republic's ban on divorce. |
| 1987 | Eleven killed before Enniskillen service on Remembrance Sunday. |
| 1989 | Fianna Fáil form coalition government for the first time in their history following general election. Their partners are the Progressive Democrats. Charles Haughey remains Taoiseach. |
| 1990 | Republic of Ireland reach quarter-finals of the soccer world cup in Italy under the management of Jack Charlton. |
| 1990 | Mary Robinson elected seventh President of Ireland, the first woman to hold the office. |
| 1992 | Dr. Eamon Casey, bishop of Galway, flees country after it was revealed that he had fathered a child in the course of an affair nearly twenty years previously. The first of a succession of sexual scandals that eroded the authority of the Catholic Church in the course of the decade |
| 1994 | IRA and Loyalist paramilitary groups announce ceasefire. |
| 1996 | In the Republic of Ireland, a constitutional referendum to permit civil divorce and re-marriage is carried narrowly. |
| 1996 | End of IRA ceasefire. |
| 1997 | Following Labour victory in British general election, Dr. Marjorie (Mo) Mowland appointed first woman Secretary of State for Northern Ireland. |
| 1997 | Fianna Fáil-PD coalition under Bertie Ahern replaces Rainbow coalition (Fine Gael, Labour, Democratic Left) following general election in the Republic. |
| 1997 | IRA declare a resumption of the 1994 ceasefire (July). |

# Further Reading

Aalen, F. H. A., Kevin Whelan & Matthew Stout (eds), *Atlas of the Irish Rural Landscape,* Cork University Press, 1997.

Andrews, J. H., *Ireland in Maps,* Dolmen Press, 1961.

Bagwell, Richard, *Ireland Under the Tudors,* Longman, 1885–90. *Ireland Under the Suarts,* Longman, 1909–16.

Bardon, Jonathan, *A History of Ulster,* Blackstaff, 1992.

Barnard, T. C., *Cromwellian Ireland: English Government and Reform in Ireland, 1649–60,* Clarendon Press, 1975.

Bradshaw, Brendan, *The Irish Constitutional Revolution of the Sixteenth Century,* Cambridge University Press, 1979.

Brown, Terence, *Ireland: a Social and Cultural History, 1922–79,* Fontana, 1981.

Buckland, Patrick, *A History of Northern Ireland,* Gill and Macmillan, 1981.

Byrne, F. J., *Irish Kings and High-Kings,* Batsford, 1973.

Canny, Nicholas P., *The Elizabethan Conquest of Ireland: A Pattern Established, 1565–76,* Harvester Press, 1976.

Curtis, Edmund, *A History of Medieval Ireland,* Barnes and Noble, 1983.

de Paor, Máire and Liam, *Early Christian Ireland,* Thames & Hudson, 1978.

Duffy, Seán, *Ireland in the Middle Ages,* Gill and Macmillan, 1997.

Ellis, Steven G., *Tudor Ireland: Crown, Community and the Conflict of Cultures, 1470–1603,* Longman, 1985.

Foster, R. F. , *Modern Ireland, 1600–1972,* Penguin, 1988. (ed) *The Oxford Illustrated History of Ireland,* Oxford University Press, 1989.

Gillespie, Raymond, *Colonial Ulster: The Settlement of East Ulster, 1600–1641,* Cork University Press, 1985.

Harbison, Peter, *Pre Christian Ireland*, Thames & Hudson, 1988. (ed) *The Shell Guide to Ireland*, Macmillan, 1989.

Kelly, James, *Prelude to Union: Anglo-Irish Politics in the 1780s*, Cork University Press, 1992.

Kinealy, Christine, *This Great Calamity, The Irish Famine, 1845-52*, Gill & Macmillan, 1994.

Lee, Joseph, *Ireland, 1912–85*, Cork University Press, 1989.

Lennon, Colm, *Sixteenth-Century Ireland*, Gill and Macmillan, 1994.

Lydon, James, *The Lordship of Ireland in the Middle Ages*, Gill and Macmillan, 1972.

Lyons, F. S. L. (ed), *Ireland since the Famine*, Fontana, 1973.

Meeham, Bernard, *The Book of Kells*, Thames & Hudson, 1994.

Mitchell, Frank, *The Shell Guide to Reading the Irish Landscape*, Country House, 1986.

Moody, T. W., F. X. Martin and J. F. Byrne (eds), *A New History of Ireland*, 9 vols, Clarendon Press, 1976–.

Ó Corráin, Donncha, *Ireland before the Normans*, Gill and Macmillan, 1972.

O'Kelly, M. J., *Early Ireland*, Cambridge University Press, 1989.

Orpen, G. H., *Ireland under the Normans*, 4 vols, Oxford University Press, 1912–20.

O'Ríordáin, S. P., *Antiquities of the Irish Countryside*, Methuen, 1979.

Otway-Ruthven, A. J., *A History of Medieval Ireland*, Ernest Benn, 1968, 1980.

Stalley, Roger, *The Cistercian Monasteries of Ireland*, Yale University Press, 1987.

Woodham-Smith, Cecil, *The Great Hunger*, Hamish Hamilton, 1987.

# Index

References in this index in bold face are for maps or pictures

# Acknowledgments

THE PUBLISHERS would like to thank to following for the photographs and illustrations produced in this atlas:

Peter Newark's Historical Pictures, Bath, England: 14, 24, 26, 28, 35, 50, 52, 53, 56, 60, 62, 64, 66, 68, 71, 73, 78, 82, 90, 92, 94, 96, 102.
Other photographs and illustrations:
Con Brogan
Industrial Development Agency of Ireland
National Gallery of Ireland
National Library of Ireland
National Museum of Ireland
Private Collections
Trinity College, Dublin

For Arcadia Editions Limited:

Design and Cartography: Peter Gamble
                        Elsa Gibert
                        Isabelle Lewis
                        Jeanne Radford
                        Malcolm Swanston
                        Jonathan Young

Editorial: Shirley Ellis
           Andrew Lavender
           Elizabeth Wyse

Illustration: Peter Massey
              Peter Smith

Typesetting: Jeanne Radford